W9-BYL-044

God's Law

or

Man's Law

THE FUNDAMENTALIST CHALLENGE
TO SECULAR RULE

Laina Farhat-Holzman

Printed in the United States of America
ISBN: 1-932053-05-0
Book design by Z-N

Library of Congress Control Number: 2005921976

NONE
THE
LESS
PRESS

http://www.nonethelesspress.com

10   9   8   7   6   5   4   3   2   1

I dedicate this book to my husband, whose encouragement and good sense kept me focused. I thank my good friend and colleague, Ed Fisher, a mathematician, whose logical mind was employed in critiquing the first edition manuscript. I also thank Morten Nilsen, my editor and typographer, for the marvelous improvements he and his eight-kilogram Siberian cat have made in this edition. And most essentially, I dedicate this book to friends around the world who cherish our democratic institutions. Theocracy is a bad idea whose time is past.

CONTENTS

Biblical literalism seemed to be on the decline since the famous
Scopes trial in the 1920s. It is once more a force and is enjoying
favor in our current government.

What happens when religious law supplants secular law can be seen
in Iran, Afghanistan, Sudan, Pakistan, and Nigeria.

A number of secular states: Algeria, Egypt, Israel, Turkey, Pakistan,
India, Malaysia, Indonesia, Nigeria, and to a lesser degree others,
have experienced serious challenges to secular rule. Some of these
countries are losing the struggle.

Education is apparently not enough to prevent people from being
lured into cults with horrifying agendas. There are serious problems
in Japan, the United States, and Europe with cult recruitment.

CONTENTS

Church and State

Under an oak in stormy weather
I joined this rogue and whore together;
And none but he who rules the thunder
Can put this rogue and whore asunder.
—Anonymous

Introduction

T his book, first written in the late 1990s, was intended to provide an overview of what I then perceived to be a new global problem: militant religious conservatism. Just before publication, America was attacked by Muslim radicals on September 11, 2001. Suddenly, what had originally been a survey of a near-term religious/political trend became much more current and specific. While all militant religions present problems, militant Islam has become a real danger to the world—and is even at war with mainstream Islam.

Only a few years ago, the prospect of a backward, literalist sect taking on the modern world would have seemed ridiculous. We have at our disposal every advanced technology—economic, medical, and military—while they have nothing but an ancient text, selectively interpreted, and a raging death cult.

However, we overlooked that people can have medieval minds, yet can manage such important technologies as modern communications, ordnance, and, potentially, weapons of mass destruction. This enemy uses terrorism as a tactic, but it apparently has a political aim that resembles nothing more than fascism. They have a goal of taking control of the lives of 1 billion Muslims, and, after that, taking the rest of us on.

Of course this goal is delusional, but they are making life for millions of people grim indeed. It appears to me that we are now living in an era that will host a new religious war, akin to the wars that began in the sixteenth century in Europe. Those wars were so devastating that they gave rise to something new in the world: the belief that church and state must be separate and that religions must be tolerant to each other. The modern world upholds this view, and even the United States, which has more religiosity than other modern nations, cannot secure state support for any one sect.

Islam, however, is a younger religion than Christianity or Judaism, and it appears that it is now ripe for religious wars and badly needed reformation. Globalization of the world has progressed so much that what once would have been a regional problem is now universal. Like it or not, we cannot escape being in the middle of Islam's agony.

Who would have imagined that religion would be the trigger for World War IV?

As a professor of World History, I used to look at religion in the same way that I regarded any other historic institution—as something linear. Looking back over the 5,000 years of recorded history, it seemed as if human values evolved, if not in a straight line, at least in an upward-moving spiral. And yes, it seemed upward (hence better) to me.

Just as we have seen a political trajectory from the ancient God-Kings to universal suffrage, we have also seen the religious transformation from human sacrifice and fear-based superstition to a benign spirituality as exemplified by the scientifically perceived ecology movement and the spiritually based United Nations Universal Declaration of Human Rights.

I assumed that with education, everyone in the world would enter that enlightened realm of benign religion. It was just a matter of time.

When the gates of hell clanged shut, said one wag in the nineteenth century, the gates of heaven also closed. He assumed that one could not cherry-pick in religion without killing it. Gone were human sacrifice, divination by "reading" the entrails of sacrificed animals, the wild-eyed prophets leading people into death and destruction, the notion that people could be possessed by demons, and the evil eye, I thought.

Although I had thought these things were gone, my daily ventures into newspapers and the popular media (well before 9/11) have disabused me of this belief. None of these ancient curses are gone; nor are they just living in the still unenlightened parts of this planet. They are next door, down the street, and in some political organizations in this country, as well as armed and dangerous in other places around the world. We had the bold return of religiously provoked suicide/murder in the horrifying terrorist attack on New York and Washington on September 11, 2001. This batch of killers had some sort of Western education.

It is alarming that Western education has not accomplished the desired end of bringing reason and enlightenment to the world. Until now, I have assumed that the cure for irrational religious beliefs rests in education. Apparently it does not—or perhaps education is not doing the job of teaching people how to think critically. Could it be possible for one's mind to be divided into the rational and the irrational at the same time? The Arab hijackers are not alone in this.

For example, many of us watched with disbelief as the very educated president of South Africa, Mr. Mbeki, stubbornly dismissed modern science in his pronouncement that AIDS does not come from the HIV virus. Then, when I saw an article about persecution of "witches" in South Africa (December 2000), I began to suspect another dynamic going on here.

The modern South African government has put a stop to what was nothing less than annual pogroms against women accused of witchcraft in rural South Africa. The locals believed that lightning strikes that set thatched roofs afire were the work of witches. I am not surprised at such ignorance from peasants with long, bad traditions, but was shocked to learn that a local medical doctor who was trained in England supported the witchcraft thesis, as did the chief of the regional police, a university-educated and multi-lingual intellectual. Could it be that President Mbeki, as educated as he is, also believes in witchcraft? Perhaps witchcraft, not HIV, produces AIDS? [*CSM*, 12/6/00]

At the point that I was ready to cast South Africa into the nether lands of incurable ignorance, another article caught my eye. The people in a county in Kentucky that one could only call backwoods (high rate of illiteracy and its corresponding poverty) protested the building of a new library offered by the state. The people did not see the need for a library that would be of no use to anybody. "We have the Bible," said their spokesman, "and that is good enough for us."

The fanatics being trained in "Islamic Schools" in Pakistan have no more in their education than memorizing the Koran in a language they cannot understand. Like their counterparts in Kentucky, they think the Koran is good enough for them. Yet they happily embrace the hope of using advanced nuclear technology to blow away their enemies (as well as themselves). The bomb is a gift of Allah and it should be used in their jihad, the young students say. [Goldberg, 36]

The Iranian Revolution seemed an exotic issue in 1979, the first howl of medieval religion fighting back against the modern secular world. Since then, however, many other medieval throwbacks have climbed out of their marginalized cupboards and have challenged the hard-won values that we all thought were finally mainstream. And they challenge us with the fruits of our own scientific and techno-logical achievements.

The late Ayatollah Khomeini, who professed the belief that the modern world was a satanic abomination, nonetheless sought out the latest weapons of war when his country was threatened by Iraq. He also employed an Austrian heart surgeon when he was ailing, rather than depending upon prayer or talismans.

Today, the medieval Shiite clerics, who have kept Iran in thrall since their 1979 revolution, are as two-minded as their late leader. They still want the latest weapons of mass destruction and modern medicine for their own power elite, yet they have debated such arcane spiritual issues as: if the state cuts off the hand of a thief, does the hand belong to the thief or to the state? The answer they came up with was that the hand belongs to the state, because the thief might run to a hospital and have it reattached. [Nafisi]

The problem is that when these religious reactionaries prevail, as they have in Iran, Afghanistan, and increasingly in Pakistan, the fruits of the modern world die with them. Modern science depends upon free thought and open investigation. All the answers are not found in one book.

The following are some serious quarrels between the secular and religious worlds and their effects can be devastating:

- The secular world believes in freedom of thought and con-science; ultra-orthodox (or fundamentalist) religions believe all truth is already known and is housed in their holy texts.
- Scientific skepticism and questioning conventional truths

are key to modern life; fundamentalism attacks such processes as irreverent and at war against God.

- The rights of people to equality under secular law, regardless of class, gender, or ethnicity are the hallmark of modern life and law. To fundamentalists, separation of peoples is mandated on these very bases. Caste is alive and well.
- Under secular law, women have achieved citizenship in all ways equal with men. With all fundamentalists, women are either lesser or subordinated, as in the recent ruling of the Southern Baptists, or are totally segregated, as with Islamists and ultra-Orthodox Jews. To all the ultra-pious, women are only vessels of new life and should have no say over how their bodies are used.
- Homosexuality is increasingly regarded as genetically determined in modern society, not an issue of "lifestyle" or "choice." All religious fundamentalists consider it is sin and some think it should be punished by death.

Around the world, formerly marginalized religions, not just Islam, are making war against the secular world, and it is already clear that the battles of the future will not be between nation states but rather within them, particularly in those vulnerable states that are in the process of modernizing. In such places, the gap between the educated elite and the masses of ignorant or illiterate is enormous, and that presents a great danger. Nor can the elite be trusted to defend modern values.

Pakistan, now more than fifty years old, began as a secular state modeled after British parliamentary governance, intended as a safe homeland for Muslim Indians. Today it is a state falling apart, and the secular nature of the country is shrinking daily. There are now battles to the death between and among Muslim sects. Education for the masses is nonexistent; freedom of thought earns death threats and assassinations, and the population explosion threatens survival altogether. The only thing holding it together is a tireless, secular dictator.

Israel, also more than fifty years old, began as did Pakistan: as a safe homeland for Jews, both secular and religious. Today the secular Israelis, who have been reluctant to challenge the benefits enjoyed by the religious factions, are chafing under ultra-Orthodox bullying. Former

President Barak pointed out in exasperation that now is the time to reclaim freedom and secular governance before it is lost altogether.

India, whose beginnings were like Pakistan's and whose founding fathers were the secular, British-educated Nehru and the universalist, British-educated Gandhi (who once said that he was Hindu, Muslim, Jew, and Christian), has had serious problems with fundamentalist Hinduism and a revolt of the Untouchables.

These fundamentalist sects all over the world are not just reactionary, they also breed murder. Both Egypt and Israel lost leaders to fundamentalist fanatics. And in the West, abortion clinics have been assaulted and doctors and nurses murdered by fanatics who think they have a monopoly on truth.

Even among the educated and seemingly modern sector, strange sorts of religion can take over. How has education helped to protect young people from the irrational and positively brainless following of gurus who lure university students into cults? For a hair-raising tour down death-and-disaster lane, you might read Robert J. Lifton's *Destroying the World to Save It*, a book about the Aum Shinrikyo cult that used sarin nerve gas in a Tokyo subway. He charts a number of apocalyptic cults that will be part of the new global terrorism. These groups are mostly peopled by educated engineers, scientists, and other university graduates who believe their duty is to destroy the world so that our souls can be saved.

Why are so many educated people suspicious of science, but not suspicious of snake oil salesmen? Let us admit that many middle-class, educated Americans and British are superstitious and are supporting astrology, numerology, psychics, faith healers, herbalists, and tarot readers with their money. Millions of dollars are being made by televangelists and fundamentalist sects around the world. A fool and his money are soon parted, I have heard.

Where have we in the West gone wrong?

There is a left wing of religious fundamentalism, too, that should cause us concern. Some Animal Rights people and militant vegetarians and ecologists are looking cult-like and are attacking enemies of their value system. How much longer before killing will be on their agendas?

In eastern Long Island, New York, an upscale subdivision being built on old farmland was torched. Three nearly completed houses were set fire deliberately and messages were spray-painted on another house: "Stop Urban Sprawl," "If You Build It We Will Burn It," and "Burn the Rich." The group doing it is called ELF, which is well known in the Pacific Northwest for extreme environmental activism, or eco-terrorism. ELF stands for Earth Liberation Front.

There is a fellow organization: ALF, Animal Liberation Front. Their actions are growing more violent all the time. So far there have been multimillion-dollar arson destruction in a new ski resort in Vail, Colorado and a million-dollar arson fire at a lumber company's office in Monmouth, Oregon.

Initially western, they have now moved east. The FBI cannot find them, and does not know who they are. Their actions are growing more violent, and include razor-laced letters sent to people in the fur business.

The intent of this book is to survey what appears to be the next battlefield around the world: the struggle for the autonomy of men and women in democratic societies vs. those persons who take their orders from their perception of God and convince the gullible to fall in line. Although one can fall in line voluntarily, one cannot fall out of line where the forces of divine authority prevail. In non-secular societies, defection brings with it a death sentence. In secular societies, cults must resort to murder to keep their members in line. Only in the secular modern world do people have the right to choose their own leaders, their own path, and their own kind of spirituality.

It is a modern concept that spirituality is most authentic when it is voluntary. Reason without the spiritual dimension leads to empty materialism, but religion without reason leads to superstition and can turn murderous. The trick for the healthy secular society is to have both reason and spirit working together. But reason must lead.

This book will explore the following areas:
- Chapter 1: An exploration of America's Muscular Christianity: The Religious Right
- Chapter 2: Fundamentalist Challenges to Secular States (Algeria, Egypt, Israel, Nigeria, Palestine, South Africa, South- and Southeast Asia, Turkey, and others).

- Chapter 3: What happens when religious fascism takes over (Afghanistan, Iran, Sudan, Nigeria, and Pakistan,)
- Chapter 4: Cults enlisting educated followers (Japan, United States, Europe)
- Chapter 5: Cults enlisting the illiterate (US, Israel, Burma, Caribbean, Philippines, Uganda, China).
- Chapter 6: Twisted Thinking—The anti-science movements and their relationships with superstition. Problems with Western-educated third-worlders reverting to cult notions (South Africa, Malaysia, Indonesia)
- Chapter 7: A simmering problem around the religious world: the status of women.
- Chapter 8: "Earthly" issues—population explosion, ecological collapse, and geological/astronomical cataclysms and their effect on religion.
- Chapter 9: Historic Perspective and Parallels
- Epilogue: Religion as a Time Machine

Sources for much of this book have been found in the popular media. Daily newspapers, television and radio, and cinema trends have provided pictures that taken daily seem to be oddities, but cumulatively show a trend.

Several scholarly works have been essential to this project. Karen Armstrong's work, *The Battle For God*, provides historic perspective on the resurgence of militant religion in its battle against the modern world. She is far more sympathetic to their wounded feelings than I am, and her conclusion that we must dialogue with these groups poses the question: how does one argue with someone whose marching orders come directly from God?

V. S. Naipal's two works, *Among the Believers* and *Beyond Belief*, represent his pilgrimage into the world of resurgent Islam. The first journey was taken in 1981, immediately after the Iranian Revolution, and the second fifteen years later, revisiting some of the people he had interviewed the first time. As always with male pilgrims to the Islamic world, none of his informants were women. Yet this sharp-eyed traveler did not miss much.

Robert J. Lifton's *Destroying the World to Save It* is a book about the Aum Shinrikyo cult that used sarin nerve gas in a Tokyo subway. He takes a hard look at how people educated in a thoroughly Western discipline—often science—can totally surrender all critical thought and become slaves of a guru with death and destruction as his agenda. He explores such cults around the developed world.

Another book that may give one pause is David Keys' *Catastrophe*, which tracks a worldwide collapse of old civilizations to the years following 535–37 CE, when a period of ecological and climatological catastrophes was launched by some as yet unknown event—possibly an enormous volcanic eruption or a comet crash. He leads the reader through the records, region by region (including the New World), of the consequences of little sunlight, droughts, floods, untimely hail and snow, and the famines and plagues and religious hysteria and political chaos that followed.

The reason that this book is important is that the nuclear winter following a nuclear war could give us a similar scenario. Though the Cold War nuclear standoff between the US and the USSR is apparently over, we still could have a serious event of this sort if India and Pakistan go at each other or if some crazy cultist launches an attack on Israel.

Jacques Barzun's final master opus, *From Dawn to Decadence*, provided a 500-year survey of Western culture. One gets perspective from such a work. Our half-millennium began in violence and ended in even worse violence—with an end to empires and the large nation-state, and the internal security that they provide.

Another book that has given me some unquiet is Jared Diamond's *Guns, Germs, and Steel,* in which he reminds us that the evolutionary trajectory is not always upward. Some societies have retreated from the agricultural revolution and gone back to hunting and gathering. Afghanistan and central Africa are beginning to look that way.

Democratic societies could lose everything if they are not vigilant. I, for one, have no desire to return to any period of human history before our own. The past has been much worse for the majority of human beings living on this planet, and if you doubt this, visit central Africa, rural Afghanistan, or the rural Andes in Peru. These places give one a good picture of the past.

And perhaps most important to those who are sincerely spiritual, religion must be free and voluntary—both to join and to leave. As the ancient Jewish scholar Hillel said: the Lord has Many Mansions.

No one faith fits all spirits. Indeed, there should also be freedom to profess no faith at all, but to live decently and honorably with all other human beings on this spaceship earth.

Laina Farhat-Holzman

February, 2005

NOTE: To make the documentation of this work less cumbersome, I list the newspapers that I have consulted (local, regional, and national) as follows:

- *Santa Cruz Sentinel* [*SCS*], my local paper, owned by Dow Jones, followed by date,
- *San Francisco Chronicle* [*SFC*], a regional centrist paper, followed by date,
- *Christian Science Monitor* [*CSM*], excellent for its international coverage, followed by date.

The reason for selecting these, rather than the "newspaper of record," the *NY Times*, is to illustrate that anyone living almost anywhere in the United States, could do the same and could be adequately informed on the social/political issues in this book.

In this text, books or major articles cited will have the author's name and relevant page number in brackets [Armstrong, 21]. The bibliography at the end of the volume will provide the full publication data and will also be annotated. I hope this will be useful to those who want to follow unfolding events.

"There's no reason to bring religion into it. I think we ought to have as great a regard for religion as we can, so as to keep it out of as many things as possible."
—Sean O'Casey, *The Plough and the Stars*

Chapter 1.
Muscular Christianity in America

Religion expert Karen Armstrong has provided an empathetic overview of a movement that is affecting every major religion—including even non-monotheistic Buddhism, Hinduism, and Confucianism. A militant piety, popularly known as "Fundamentalism," is arising everywhere, challenging governments, threatening freedom of speech and religion, and attempting to reverse the social reforms of the 20th and 21st centuries.

The manifestations of these movements include murder—murder of worshipers in a mosque in the hands of an ultra-Orthodox, ultra-nationalist Israeli; murder of abortion doctors and nurses by fundamentalist Christians; an act of terrorism in the bombing of a government building in Oklahoma; and murder of two presidents, one in Israel by an Israeli religious fanatic and one in Egypt by a Muslim fanatic. This movement has also succeeded in overturning one government by revolution (Iran) and has destroyed another country through religiously organized mayhem (Afghanistan). And since her writing, radical Islamists committed murder on a grand scale: the attack on America in September, 2001.

In China, there is an ongoing battle between the resolutely atheist government and a Christian cult that may not be as benign as it pretends.

In India and Pakistan, religion has reinvigorated the already existing enmity between Hindu and Muslim Indians, using Kashmir and rural villages as a killing ground for both sides.

These movements are characterized by literal interpretation of scripture and adherence to the strictest possible interpretation of religious law, much of it directed at women. The status of women, of course, is one of the more glaring battlefields between the secular and fundamentalist religious worlds.

This phenomenon can be seen as a consequence of change too rapid for people to make adjustments. During periods of revolutionary change, behavior does not change overnight. Throughout history, most such changes took place over a long period. It took a long time before agriculture caught on after someone in the Fertile Crescent discovered that grain could be planted and foodstuffs stored.

Nor did the world change immediately when the industrial revolution was ushered in. Some places changed, but others retained the horse plow long after the tractor was available.

What appears to be causing such violent response to the contemporary scientific and social revolutions is the rapidity of these changes and the communications and global economies that have spread these concepts everywhere.

Leo Tolstoy wrote of the peasants in his time who were hostile when their landowner introduced Brahman bulls to improve the cattle or when they bought motorized tractors. The peasants poisoned the bulls and threw stones into the engine of the tractor. They regarded any change as harmful to their interests.

Today, however, even though the reactionaries reject the scientific rationalism of the West and the social freedoms that go with it, they are quite willing to use elements of it to further their own cause. For example, although Saudi Arabia enforces a code for women that is draconian and oppressive, the government acquires the latest weapons for their military and one Saudi prince enjoyed a ride on the space shuttle. How, one wonders, did he justify the religious notion of a flat earth with what he saw with his own eyes from space?

Today we are at the cusp of the next global revolution. We are no longer a world based on agricultural surplus, which was our first revolution. We are now in a world of technological plenty. People from traditional societies are struggling to find meaning in all this change.

How does one who had no control over events, no control over the pain and misery that seemed to be one's lot, deal with choices, with plenty, and with rising expectations of a better life? What is a better life? Is it better for women to have the same freedoms as men? Who then will raise the children? Or from the man's standpoint, where have his privileges gone?

Furthermore, when the inevitable sorrow does enter one's life, where can one go to get comfort? Reason, science, and technology may not help a suffering person to come to grips with loss, pain, and sorrow. Religion has always taken on this function, and our modern world seems to have short-sheeted faith.

As Karen Armstrong notes, logos (our reasoning faculty) began to drive out mythos (our capacity for finding meaning) from the eighteenth century on, and the revolt against this has simmered for almost two centuries now.

"Fundamentalists feel that they are battling against forces that threaten their most sacred values," she says. "Modernization has led to a polarization of society. Even if we value this modernization, we must recognize that others experience it not as liberation but as aggressive assault." [Armstrong, xvi]

With the industrial revolution, the emergence of reason as the sole criterion of truth in the West also unleashed an eruption of religious irrationality. The great witch crazes, devil worship, and even the Great Awakening (the revival movement in nineteenth-century America) emerged in response to what was perceived as too much reason. [Armstrong, 71]

Armstrong's empathetic view differs from that of Frederick Clarkson in *Eternal Hostility: The Struggle Between Theocracy and Democracy*. Clarkson sees the American "Religious Right" as a conspiracy to replace democracy with their own theocracy—using democracy's own rules to do so. He does not see them as people under siege, but rather as people who are cynical and evil who intend to take power.

Armstrong is probably more correct about the feelings of the rank and file fundamentalists—but Clarkson seems to have an accurate fix on the leadership. Jerry Falwell and Pat Robertson have made that obvious in their recent pronouncement that the attack on America was God's punishment for our many "liberal" sins.

Religious revival in America

The nineteenth-century American Great Awakening, with its passionate revival meetings, met the need of people who were uprooted, were settling a land new to them, and were using new technologies that had no traditions with their use. There was too much "logos" and not enough "mythos." Egalitarian, fundamentalist Christianity filled the void.

By the 1920s, it appeared that this muscular Christianity settled down into the poorer, more backward sections of the country, a belt that crossed the south and ended in the southwest, called the "Bible Belt." A telling conflict between that world and the increasingly secular America came to a head in a notorious court case, the Scopes "Monkey" trial in Tennessee.

A young biology teacher was being prosecuted for attempting to teach Darwin's theory of evolution in a high school biology class. The prosecution, representing Christian fundamentalism and the biblical story of creation, won the case in Tennessee, but lost the battle across the nation.

The press covered this case and had great fun commenting on what they perceived as country bumpkins. It appeared that the majority of Americans preferred to take their religion symbolically rather than literally, thereby finding no conflict between Bible stories and modern science. The Bible Belt licked its wounds, retreated, and waited for an opportunity.

After the 1979 Islamic Revolution in Iran, it appeared that the lid came off of the submerged fundamentalists around the world. V. S. Naipal, a remarkably astute world traveler and citizen of the world (he is of East Indian origin and a citizen of Jamaica), took a journey through the non-Arab Muslim world from Iran to Indonesia to see why people were marching quickstep back into medievalism. [Naipal, *Among the Believers*]

His findings will be discussed later when we survey Islam. However, one significant element emerged in his interviews: the new enthusiasts for fundamentalism (all male) made note of the satisfaction of putting women back in their place. The secular world's emancipation of women seems to have created enormous resentment among such men.

Political Christianity

In the United States, upon the election of Ronald Reagan and the aftermath of the Islamic Revolution, resentments surfaced among people who had felt marginalized. Along with the conservative election sweep of Mr. Reagan came the election of a number of people from the Bible Belt who were no longer willing to suppress their beliefs.

According to Karen Armstrong, the new Christian Right took on feminism, Marxism, humanism, all of which they saw as the philosophy of death, death of an entire civilization represented by what they imagined as "the good old days."

Protestant fundamentalists and Catholic and Mormon conservatives seem to have felt "unmanned" by the evil forces of secular humanism. Male fear of impotence became a big issue, which may explain the hatred for homosexuality. Many thought that Christianity had become a religion of womanly values: forgiveness, mercy, and tenderness. They preferred the Christianity of the Crusades, particularly since the Muslims were resurrecting the other side of that exciting time. [Armstrong, 312]

Some groups of radical Christians, happily not yet in power, simmered in the fringes of American civilization—in Montana and Idaho or in the eastern backwoods. They are not just "survivalists," but are "reconstructionists," training themselves for the day that they can take over the country and set things right. They are preparing to do so by force, and there have already been some conflicts between the federal government and these armed-to-kill radicals. [Armstrong, 361]

Incredible as it may seem, the Reconstructionists believe in overturning all modern secular jurisdiction and replace it with the law of the Old Testament—which they consider all the constitution that our society needs. Death penalties would once more include stoning adulteresses and women unchaste before marriage, as well as the death penalty for apostasy, heresy, blasphemy, homosexuality, idolatry, witchcraft, striking a parent, incorrigible juvenile delinquency, abortion, and other things that would be right at home in today's Islamic Republic of Iran, where stoning recently was revived.

It is interesting that the Reconstructionists would also resurrect the modes of capital punishment found in the Bible: burning at the stake, stoning, and death by the sword. [Clarkson, 81] What amazes me is that this movement has a following!

It is important to note that this sort of movement, although it appears backward, is very modern. It believes in centralized dictatorship, modern military technology, exclusion, hatred, and violence. Fear lies barely beneath the surface. One hears stories of all sorts of international conspiracies to take over the United States, such as the (imaginary) fleet of black helicopters with which the United Nations will occupy this country by force.

In the mainstream of elected fundamentalists, best characterized by former Congressman Newt Gingrich's "Contract With America," the agenda was less paranoid, yet extremely far reaching. There was open warfare against the feminization of modern society. Although they could not take away women's suffrage, they could try to take away abortion rights and certainly make a dent in affirmative action.

Racism and sexism became once more issues that could be uttered aloud—in jokes, in conversations, and on the airwaves and Internet. Feminists could be called "femi-Nazis" with impunity. Anger at desegregation by state edict could once more be expressed through antibussing demonstrations and waving the Confederate flag.

Passionate opposition emerged (selectively) toward medical intervention—selecting intervention when it saves soldier's lives, heart attack and stroke victims, but rejecting it when the intervention might result in death (pulling the plug in vegetative coma, or late term abortion of an encephalic baby). It has also been noticed that the most ardent opponents of abortion are ardent supporters of capital punishment.

American Catholicism

American Catholicism has not only survived the Protestant bigotry of the 19th and early 20th centuries, but has overcome much of this former antipathy. Catholicism plays an important role in American life, but a role that is undergoing transformation and fragmentation.

Gone are the days when the cinema industry lived in fear of a film being put on the Catholic banned list. Also gone are the days when a state such as Connecticut could be bullied by the Church into banning contraceptive information to adult women.

However, there is a new alliance between conservative Catholic forces and their Protestant fundamentalist counterparts in opposing abortion and birth control, and anything that looks like compassionate euthanasia for the terminally ill. This union makes for a powerful political force. Although the majority of Americans do not agree with these positions, this majority is not heard as much as the conservative alliance.

On the liberal side of Catholicism, increasingly alienated from old-line Catholics, there is a movement to end capital punishment and there is a movement of resolute pacifism. For these causes, such liberal Catholics ally with liberal Protestants, Reform Jews, and a few moderate American Muslims. The Religious Ecumenical Movement is made up of such liberal interpreters of religion—genuine fundamentalists see this movement as another enemy.

Homegrown religions

The religious diversity permitted in this country has given rise to at least two totally homegrown religions: Christian Science and The Church of Jesus Christ of Latter Day Saints (Mormons). The former also has the distinction of being the first religion founded by a woman with a following that is not just feminine.

Christian Science is founded on the principle that the body is healthy and self-regulating, and that much day-to-day illness is of mental (or spiritual) origin. This insight is probably not incorrect. The religion takes this view to an extreme, however, in believing that prayer can heal everything. Every so often, parents are prosecuted by the state when one of their children dies unnecessarily, and the issue of "freedom of religion" comes up.

The Church of Jesus Christ of Latter Day Saints has an even stranger history. Much persecuted during its formative years during the period of the Protestant Great Awakening, the Mormon sect migrated to Utah and created a unique society there, which has, over time, become respectable and powerful.

To the casual observer, the culture of Mormonism has produced solid, law-abiding communities that value hard work and believe in taking care of their own needy. The community has protected itself by officially acceding to US law by ending polygamy, a tenet of early Mormonism. In return for being granted statehood, they officially abandoned this practice (although unofficially it still thrives in fringe areas).

This sect has also guaranteed its future by institutionalizing missionary efforts to recruit more people into their religion. Every young man must serve several years as a missionary—often going to very remote parts of the world for this effort. Mormonism is growing.

A closer look at Mormonism brings less cheery elements to view. There is a very strange theology that involves other worlds, the idea that the dear departed may become gods (which makes some wonder how monotheistic this cult is), and a strong apocalyptic belief that the end is near. Mormons have official and private supply depots for the time that the world begins its horrifying descent into destruction. [*Time Magazine*, 8/4/97] There may be a connection here with the cults of survivalists—many of whom live in Mormon areas—who are armed and ready for the end of America, if not the end of the world.

The official Mormon establishment quietly looks the other way at Mormon cults for whom illegal polygamy is a "divine principle," even though this practice has become a financial burden on the state of Utah. Welfare pays for this clandestine practice because the majority of people living this way live in near poverty.

Polygamy is a system that breeds population explosion with all the attendant ills that accompany it. In addition, there is the problem of choice, a serious American value. Does a teenage girl have a choice when she is handed over by her polygamous parents to become one more plural wife of another polygamist? There have been several recent court cases on this very issue, as well as on serious issues of battery and child sexual abuse.

In Colorado City, Arizona, Mormons are pulling their children out of public schools and cutting off communications with outsiders and former church members. [*SCS*, 9/17/2000] The Mormon Church has been looking the other way as fringe polygamy continued in Utah and Arizona. Word has it that one big issue is the Second Coming of Christ. These fundamentalists are very apocalyptic, in addition to their strange conviction that polygamy is a "principle" that they are willing to defend "to their death."

The twilight zone

Because the United States is such an open society for religion, that is, because it has been blessed by having no "established church," it is also a nursery for a bizarre range of cults and for private practices that defy reason. These will be taken up in more detail in Chapter 5, Cults Recruiting the Ignorant.

Popular culture as exemplified by cinema and television dramas and talk shows has taken up what seems to be an obsession with angels and devils. The media fascination with Satan has been somewhat tongue-in-cheek, as in the film *The Devil's Advocate*, in which the devil runs a law firm. The interest in angels has been much more serious, as in the popular television drama *Touched By An Angel*. Even the actors in this show profess belief in the reality of angels.

On thirteen acres of land near Santa Cruz, California, residents claim that people have walked out of the woods cured of cancer; that alcoholics have left with their thirst dried up; that people with hepatitis have had it squeezed out of their livers like water from a sponge. "It's the angels at work," they say, and it began when a man saw the vision of an angel while cutting wood on the property. When the vision faded, it left behind its image on a six-inch oak log. The angels told a forty-two-year-old medium named Crystal that it was time to contact the media." [*SCS*, July 18, 1999]

Of more concern are the cults hidden in pockets of this country that take a far more sinister approach to this mythology. When a mother and daughter in New York City beat their mentally retarded daughter/sibling to death "to drive out the devil," or when an educated American who is now a Santorean priest ritually sacrifices a chicken to bless a parishioner's car, we are in the Twilight Zone.

Literal interpretations

There have been numerous cases in which seemingly modern couples, obviously educated, take their biblical interpretation literally and use prayer and anointing with oil rather than surgery, resulting in the needless deaths of children with treatable ailments, such as, for example, a ruptured appendix.

This from Alabama: "If the Rev. James Henderson has his way, the division of church and state in this tiny hamlet [Brooksville, Alabama] will be so narrow, a single Bible verse, 'Love thy neighbor,' would cover it." [SFC, 1/2/99] The rest of the article is about a group of residents who want to form a town, "but not one in which mortal elected officials would have the power to hand out liquor licenses, levy taxes and rezone land for strip malls and industrial parks."

They want a town governed by the hand of God. The King James Bible would be the town charter, the Ten Commandments its ordinances. Voting—infrequent voting—would be done in church. This is obviously in league with the Reconstructionists, but is even more ignorant.

In another case, a California father, John Davis, said God and the Bible instructed him to be strict with his children so they wouldn't grow up to kill him and his wife. "Proverbs tells you to discipline your children, or else they will grow up and kill their parents," Davis said. "All I did was discipline them." His notion of discipline was to keep his three adolescent sons chained to their beds for years on end. His abused children responded by trying to commit suicide. [SCS, 10/24/00]

One youngster succeeded. He died after eating some drywall (and before he could be taken to a doctor, Davis said.) His body was burned in a trash bag. Another boy escaped and went to the police, upon which the parents were arrested. The boys were malnourished, underdeveloped and scarred from whippings, and also had marks on their wrists from restraints. The father later committed suicide in jail. [SCS, 3/11/01]

In another case, a nationwide manhunt ended after searchers found a malnourished child at a remote campsite in Montana, where his parents, claiming he was the Christ Child, were hiding him after allegedly kidnapping him from a Utah hospital, an FBI spokesman said. He was hospitalized for severe malnutrition; twenty months old and weighing what a six-month-old would weigh. "Relatives said David (their twenty-month-old baby) was fed a diet of lettuce and watermelon to keep his body pure because his parents believed he was either the Christ Child or a prophet." [SFC, 10/6/98]

Apocalyptic cults abound, particularly because of our self-invented counting system. New Year of 2000 and 2001 gave rise to millennial madness with people who believe that the end was near. The following cases were widely publicized.

A cult in southern California that supported itself through providing computer services (which indicates the level of education of its members) committed group suicide in the belief that a space ship was nearby and would take them all to a better world.

The horrifying end of both Jim Jones' San Francisco cult, which ended in murder and mass suicide in Guiana, and the David Koresh cult in Waco, Texas, which ended in a shootout with federal agents and a fire set by cult leaders, are but the tip of the iceberg. Other cults around the country will continue to flourish until they too have disastrous ends. All of these cults are apocalyptic.

One cult in New York state has self-appointed "prophets" among their leadership. One of these prophets mandated the starvation death of one cult baby, and several other little bodies have been unearthed by the authorities. [*SFC*, 11/14/00]

The leader of a fundamentalist sect and his wife in Bedford, Massachusetts, were indicted on murder charges in the death of their infant son, who, authorities believe, died of starvation. A third member of the sect was charged as an accessory. This sect does not believe in modern medicine or our legal system. A father turned states evidence and blew the whistle, leading authorities to the graves of this baby and his own child. They believed that a "vision" of one of their members, a "prophet," told them to starve the baby. They would walk by his crib and watch his eyes roll in his head and see his ribs and then go eat dinner. Who knows how many other such cults go unnoticed and do their harm in the dark? [*SFC* 11/14/00]

Cult of the Virgin

A major movement is afoot that many might not put in the "Twilight Zone" category, but I believe it belongs there. The Cult of the Virgin Mary was forced on the reluctant Catholic Church in the tenth century CE by a public that simply was not ready to give up the great Mother Goddess.

According to newspaper accounts, worldwide hysterical sightings of the Virgin Mary are on the increase. [*SFC*, 12/25/98] The approach of the millennium, the strong Marian devotion of Pope John Paul II, and the continuing influence of events at Medjugorje, a Bosnian village where the mother of Jesus supposedly appeared in 1981, have all stimulated this passion.

Several years ago in Conyers, Georgia, 100,000 people gathered to hear Nancy Fowler, a housewife who purports to channel messages from the Virgin Mary.

In another incident, 500 people and a couple of priests ignored the warnings of Archbishop William Levada and turned out to see Vassula Ryden, a pseudo-Catholic channel, at the Herbst Theater in San Francisco. She claims to receive divine messages from Jesus, Mary and an angel named Daniel, and writes them down in elegant script—the books are doing a brisk business. Her message is becoming more apocalyptic lately. Vassula has also added a faith healing service to her performance.

The Church doesn't like it. (One may wonder if the problem is that it is a woman preaching, a woman who is a former fashion model born in Egypt to Greek parents). The churchmen claim that these messages are not divine revelations, but personal meditations, containing elements that are negative in the light of Church doctrine.

In yet another incident, two dozen Mexican farm workers and their families gathered around a large shade tree at a Yuba City, California housing project. They saw an image of Mary in a large knothole and have laid candles and poinsettias at the base of the tree. The same sort of sighting took place in the Hispanic community of Watsonville near Santa Cruz, California not long after.

At the very respectable San Francisco Grace Cathedral, Reverend Alan Jones, dean of the cathedral, is leading a pilgrimage to Chartres Cathedral titled "Mary and the Birth of the Soul." He claims that Mary is part of a broader shift from dogma to imagery in American religion, a revival more emotional than intellectual. Indeed it is.

Professor Mark Miravalle of the Franciscan University in Steubenville, Ohio, is the leader of another popular Marian movement. [*SFC*, 12/24/00] He is leading a campaign to have Pope John Paul recognize the Virgin as Co-redeemer with Jesus. He was much taken by an event in Bosnia about a decade ago, when several small children received a visit from the Virgin. Professor Miravalle did his doctoral dissertation on the messages that the Virgin Mary gave the Bosnian children who first saw her. She reportedly told the children that she opposes abortion, birth control, female priests, and communism. To Miravalle, the three cornerstones of her messages are "prayer, penance and fasting." He believes that the world of today is in desperate need of a mother. The conveniently conservative message from the Virgin is apt to receive the Pope's support.

A testimony to the ecumenical nature of the American twilight zone was an incident a few years ago in San Francisco. A portable cement traffic barrier post fell off a truck and was "planted" in Golden Gate Park by a bystander, only to find gifts of food and flowers deposited to honor what someone now perceives as "the lingam of the God Shiva." The traffic barrier immediately became a focal point for planeloads of reverent pilgrims, a phenomenon I personally witnessed.

Consequences

Most of this subterranean and even mainstream religiosity in America has not had as major a consequence for us as religion has elsewhere in the world. However, these phenomena cannot be ignored either, because the more powerful among the religious leaders may attempt to use them to manipulate our political, as well as our social, values.

One facet of the Fundamentalist resurgence in America has been the quiet takeover of boards of education and PTAs, the consequences of which nobody noticed until almost too late. In 1999, the Kansas State Board of Education, which had been infiltrated by Christian fundamentalists, managed to strike the teaching of evolution, plate tectonics, and the Big Bang theory from the science curriculum. They wanted these theories replaced or to have Biblical Creationism taught as equally valid. [*SFC*, 2/15/01] This issue apparently did not die with the notorious Scopes trial.

Kansas voters in the 2000 Republican primary election defeated the three conservative members of the school board who had perpetrated this action and science was back in the curriculum. However, the conservatives are back on the board and, instead of creationism, the new wording is "Intelligent Design."

The consequences of this Creationism movement are the degradation of education in Kansas and the inabilityof students to get into respectable universities. A key facet of being an educated person is basic comprehension of science and knowledge of the difference between "logos" and "mythos." Fundamentalists have contaminated these two modes of knowing.

An even more serious alliance is in the works as I write. The Reverend Sun Myung Moon, whose cult is known as "Moonies," is spending some of his incredible fortune on a campaign to forge an inter-faith, interracial alliance. Despite his prison term for tax evasion, his movement during recent decades has financed extensive business ventures around the world, including *The Washington Times* and United Press International and a range of other networks. [Clarkson, Chapter 3]

The common denominator with other religious institutions is that they are all very conservative and essentially anti-democratic. His money has gone to Louis Farrakhan of the Nation of Islam, and to Baptist and Lutheran groups with conservative leanings. In addition, high visibility speakers have been lured by the enormous fees paid at Moonie events. Both former President George Bush and his wife Barbara spoke at such events in 1995.

Critics of Moon's approach say that this is all part of a strategy to achieve a worldwide theocracy under God and his representative on earth, Moon.

Clarkson, in an interview by *The Christian Science Monitor*, notes: "This is not a fringe group with no influence in society. This is an agency that has aligned itself with other contemporary theocratic movements, particularly in the Christian right. And Moon has been very outspoken against American democracy. Any time you have an explicitly anti-democratic or theocratic movement, one has to take that seriously." [*CSM*, 4/19/01]

As long as the United States keeps firm separation of church and state on the books and in practice, we are safe from the horrors of religious governance. By keeping state power separated from religion, and by keeping religion absolutely voluntary, we permit spirituality to have as many forms as people may want.

We Americans are a spiritual people, and many of us are forever seeking answers to the great questions of life: who are we, why are we here, what are we to do with our lives, and where do we go after death. The danger to this freedom is that determined rascals can overwhelm the judgment of ordinary people and can play upon their desire for spirituality.

Fundamentalism, with its certainty that it has all the answers, has great appeal to the spiritually needy. Cults with charismatic leaders can overwhelm with sheer magnetism people with educations that should have protected them.

The very freedom of mobility that characterizes our society has the downside of loneliness and rootlessness—a magnet for religious chicanery. We are, as human beings, both individualists and members of communities. These facets need to be carefully balanced.

There are some beacons of hope for the rational. A tiny center in Berkeley, California, is trying to douse Creationism's fire. Four full-time employees and 4,000 members comprise this new organization, the National Center for Science Education. With a phone call, the center can jump into action to mount a counterattack on Creationism in public schools.

They supply articles and pamphlets, legal advice and summaries of court cases, examples on writing letters to the editors of local papers, how to talk to reporters, phone numbers of national experts, links to dozens of organizations that can offer help, and phone numbers of other people in their state willing to get involved.

Founded in 1981, this organization is active in all fifty states. They are doing in a small way what the organized fundamentalists are doing with much more money and manpower. [*SCS*, 10/24/00]

Other groups doing like work include The Freedom From Religion Foundation (www.ffrf.org), The Council for Secular Humanism (www.secularhumanism.org), and The Committee for the Scientific Investigation of the Paranormal (www.csicop.org), whose founding members are Carl Sagan, Isaac Asimov, and Martin Gardner. All of these groups publish magazines that are informative and useful.

One last word on American religion: as long as there is secular law, law that can be changed as the times change, and law that is rationally determined by universal suffrage, religion can flourish within rational boundaries.

If we surrender our law and our religions to self-proclaimed leaders, both governance and religion suffer. With American religions, we are guided by the law of the marketplace: let the buyer beware.

Tantum religio potuit suadere malorum.
[Religion has so much power to promote evil.]
—Lucretius, ancient Rome,
from *Book 1, The Nature of Things*

Chapter 2.
Where religious fascism takes over

During the Cold War, it was American policy to support religious parties and groups as a bulwark against Marxism. Many Middle Eastern countries, such as Iran, Egypt, Jordan, and North African states, were laboring at disengaging their citizens from traditional and hopelessly reactionary religion. Public and secular education systems were being introduced or expanded and women were beginning to have their humanity and professional aspirations recognized.

However, all such radical change introduces danger to the government. In all of these countries, the governing elites were so alarmed by the possibility of revolution from the left that they began to court the right, the religious factions, as a counterbalance.

With the Cold War simmering around them, these countries chose sides. Countries with no pretensions at democracy (Syria, Iraq, and Libya, and to a lesser extent Algeria) chose the USSR as their big brother. Turkey, Iran, Jordan, and, after an unsatisfactory stint in the Russian camp, Egypt became staunch supporters and beneficiaries of the American side. Saudi Arabia was no contest. Its oil wealth mandated its orientation to the West, and the West overlooked its dreadful human rights record.

All of these countries have abusive human rights records in Western terms. It is necessary to see developing countries in context, however. As bad as their records are, they are far better than they were under their old traditional systems. Change is possible—and is possible even in Saudi Arabia.

Because of a genuine threat of revolution from a generation of younger military and university students who were impatient with the rate of change, the governments of all of these countries harassed intellectuals and the radicalized military, while bolstering the religious groups that they had tried to emasculate before.

Iran

The Iranian Revolution of 1979 changed all this. Too late, these modernizing Muslim countries recognized the enormous danger they were facing from the religious factions.

Nobody believed that an eighty-year-old Shiite "scholar" could seize control of a revolution that was begun by left-leaning intellectuals. If any of these revolutionaries had studied past revolutions, they would have known that great revolutions are always taken over by the most ruthless and most extreme factions, particularly those with charismatic leaders. But leftist revolutionaries are not as bright as one would hope. (The book to read is Crane Brinton, *Anatomy of a Revolution*.)

Iran today has endured almost three decades of religious fascism, with a foundering economy despite its oil wealth, and pariah status because of some very bad behavior in violating international norms and supporting terrorist training.

Holding American diplomats hostage for 444 days during the early 1980s and well-documented financial and military support for other religious fascist groups (such as Hezbollah in Lebanon) throughout the Middle East have undone much of the goodwill and modernizing development under the late Pahlavi shahs.

One process that the Ayatollah Khomeini thought that he and his colleagues could control was elections. Elections—flawed and corrupt but elections nevertheless—had been held in Iran for decades. The late Shah had enraged religious fanatics by adding women to the rolls of voters for the first time in 1963.

The Ayatollah continued the electoral process and did not even attempt to remove women from the rolls because he was certain that the clerics could control these elections and these women. They seemed to believe that because women were the most ignorant sector of the society, they would also be the most religious.

His fallback position, should things not go his way, was that he could veto anything and remove from the lists of candidates any that he deemed "un-Islamic." Iran had, and still has, a very ineffectual democracy.

However, in recent years, particularly since Khomeini's death, voters have grown more insistent. By an overwhelming mandate in 1997, the long-suffering Iranian public, a public that is two-thirds under age thirty, elected a relatively reasonable "moderate" president, a cleric, Mohammad Khatemi. Khatemi has been doing his best to loosen the stranglehold of the right wing Shiite establishment, but, in truth, he has been frustrated at every turn because he does not have real power.

Even when the moderates won overwhelmingly in the election of 1999, the reactionaries who control the courts overturned Khatami's efforts at securing press freedom. In addition, the religious cabal has evidently conducted a decade-long clandestine campaign to silence intellectual critics, including multiple assassinations.

In December 2000, eighteen officials from Iran's intelligence agency went on trial for the 1998 murders of five dissident writers and intellectuals. The Intelligence Ministry says they were "rogue" agents, whose actions were unknown to higher-ups.

Reformers say that the case exposes only a fraction of a complex, state-sponsored killing machine that has murdered as many as eighty political opponents in the past decade. They claim that this exercise has been conducted by a conspiracy of senior clerics and right wing politicians who are now engaged in a massive cover-up.

Even if these agents are found guilty by the court, the problem of Iran's governance by religious fascists who can checkmate the elected president is not resolved. [*SFC*, 12/23/00]

To make matters worse, eight of Iran's best-known dissidents have received prison sentences for attending a conference in Berlin, which the authorities said "harmed Iran's image." This is a new twist on "un-Islamic," it seems, and it is enough to confine one to a very nasty prison indeed, followed by internal exile to one of Iran's lesser garden spots. [*SFC*, 1/24/01]

Frustration is mounting among the university students, who have endured enormous harassment, and if something does not change, Iran may be close to another revolution. The revolutionaries have age on their side since the power structure is so moribund. This time, the clerics and political Islam could be overturned, but what a cost for a generation of Iranians whose progress has been thwarted.

Afghanistan

This country is the poster child for misfortune. Because of its land-locked location in Central Asia, bordering on Iran, Turkmenistan, Uzbekistan, Tajikistan, India, and Pakistan, it has been even farther out of the stream of modernization than most of its neighbors.

Afghanistan, with its culture of fierce tribalism, fanatical Islam, and belligerent, caste-ridden feudalism, illustrates all the worst facets of the past. It was, for millennia, the eastern hinterlands of Iran until the British helped foment an independence movement in the mid-nineteenth century that gave birth (on the maps) to a new country, Afghanistan.

Afghanistan's monarchy labored heroically since its inception to bring about modernization. However, it was a monarchy without military means to deal with tribes, feudal landowners, and fanatical clerics.

It is often cited by Afghans that when Kamal Ataturk, Turkey's modernizer, ordered women emancipated from the veil, there was grumbling but it happened. Then Iran's monarch, Reza Shah Pahlavi was emboldened to do the same, and he had to put down rebellion by force, but he prevailed. When the Afghan king tried to do the same thing, he was murdered. The further east one goes, apparently, the more fanatical the resistance.

The capital, Kabul, a backwater at best, was in comparison the most progressive part of Afghanistan. Countless diplomats, among them personal friends of mine, have loved and wrung their hands over poor Afghanistan. In addition, many Afghan friends now living in California have told me that Kabul was actually pleasant and like normal national capitals during the Russian occupation in the 1980s. Women were free to pursue education and professional life, and the city was full of coffee houses, cinemas, restaurants, and theaters. Since the American ouster of the Taliban, Kabul is beginning to come back to life.

Although a country without natural resources that any colonial power might covet, its location on the southern flanks of the Russian Empire and north of Britain's India made it a battleground of intrigue between the two colonial powers during the nineteenth century. It became a graveyard for foreign soldiers who could not match the ferocity and fanaticism of Afghans.

The Russians made their last try for control of Afghanistan in the 1980s, toward the end of the Cold War, and although half of Afghanistan had benefited from Soviet modernization, the other half conducted a resolute guerrilla war to drive out the "infidels." The rebels' ferocity alone would not have been enough to prevail against Soviet modern weaponry, but because of the Cold War, the US provided enough assistance to eventually drive out the Russians, an action that the world has come to rue.

The Afghan War was one factor that contributed to the demise of the Soviet Union, leaving them with veterans with a drug and demoralization problem that rags them still. It was their equivalent of our Vietnam War.

The second consequence of this war was the return of fanatical Muslim veterans of the Afghan conflict to their own countries to foment guerrilla warfare. From Algeria to Yemen and Sudan to Indonesia, one can find such veterans at the heart of every desperate venture into political chaos. Osama bin Laden had his beginnings in Afghanistan, and his movement is now global.

But the most devastating consequence of this war was for Afghanistan itself. Until invaded by the United States in 2002, to eject Al Qaeda and the Taliban government that hosted these terrorists, the country was a model of all that is worst under radical Islam.

There was no longer a monarchy or any pretense at a central modern government. Instead, there had been two decades of endless tribal warfare, "resolved" by the takeover by the most reactionary group, which calls itself the "Taliban," meaning "students." Their notion of scholarship, of course, is to memorize the Koran in a language they do not speak.

This ruling group was drawn from the countryside and received its "education" in religious schools financed by the Saudis in Pakistani refugee camps. [Kaplan and Goldberg]. Afghan specialists noted that, for all practical purposes, Pakistan seemed to have acquired a new province—the now dead Afghanistan. But it was equally possible that Afghanistan and its Taliban were spelling the demise of Pakistan. The border between the two is more theoretical than real, and the people on both sides of that border are equally fanatical and ferocious.

The Taliban's notion of proper Islam was the total persecution of women (an attitude that the Prophet Mohammad would find repellent) and the forbidding of anything (aside from modern weaponry) that smacked of the modern world and its pleasures.

The rules regarding women were strictly enforced by beatings and sometimes, if defied, death. Women were to be totally covered by a burqa, a garment with a screen through which the wearer saw the world dimly. Women could not leave their home without the company of a male relative. They could not practice their professions (teachers, judges, office workers, lawyers, university professors) because the place for women was at home, having children.

Other rules for women out-of-doors were that they must not wear white socks (too provocative) and they must wear rubber-soled flat shoes (so that they are silent when they walk). [SFC, 3/9/01]

According to the above article, Afghanistan was more civilized 1,500 years ago when it was Buddhist than under the Taliban. It had become a joyless horror. The Taliban banned everything from music to kite flying. Women were forbidden to sing or laugh aloud for fear that they might "corrupt" men. Women were beaten in the streets daily. Added to this was rape and child abuse by the very Taliban that was supposed to stop such abuses.

Women were deprived of the most elementary rights—bought and sold like cattle, humiliated, whipped, beaten, and considered to have little worth other than as a tool for satisfying males and bearing children (male children, of course).

Indoors, the lower story windows were painted over lest someone on the outside see a woman in her home.

The result of this for Afghanistan was a society so poisoned by testosterone that it represented all that was worst when men have no opposition. Despite draconian punishments, male homosexuality was the only outlet for most men. This has been true for all societies that scorn women, since the time of ancient Athens and Sparta.

The women, however, had no outlet at all. According to the UN's World Health Report of 2000, health care for women in Afghanistan was the worst in the world. Statistics on the suicide rate for these women are sketchy, but health observers thought it was very high. [*SFC*, 10/12/98] And, of course, since the majority of schoolteachers in the modern sector were women, the literacy rate for the country plummeted even lower than it was.

What passed for entertainment in Afghanistan were two activities: the first was the wild native polo-like game played with a calf's carcass (it was once the enemy's head) and the weekly Islamic punishments inflicted in the sports arena in Kabul.

Things were so dreadful in Afghanistan that even Iran, no paradise itself, called Afghanistan "medieval," and refugees poured out by the hundreds of thousands. [*SFC*, 1/10/01].

One last consequence of Afghanistan's sad and dangerous condition was that it was host to every other sort of fanatical guerrilla group, most of them religiously oriented, who were training and ready to return to their countries around the world—many of them neighbors in Central Asia—to produce more Afghanistans. The Yemeni/Saudi Arab Osama bin Laden was one such guest, and his reach extended to bombing American embassies in East Africa and eventually to an attack on the United States. The bombing of an American ship in the Gulf of Yemen in 2000 was also traced to his organization.

As the Afghan war came to a close and both the Russians and Americans left the Afghans to do what they do best, fight among themselves, Osama bin Laden had a vision. He saw a way to turn all this fanaticism into a cause—a worldwide jihad that could be directed against all the secular governments in the world, as well as those Muslim countries that were not Islamic enough.

As a historian, I am reminded of a similar situation of endless infighting during Europe's dark ages that was brought to a temporary halt by the pope, who declared the first Crusade in 1098 so that this energy could be used against the enemies of Christianity. History is cyclical.

Bin Laden's Islamic Front for Jihad Against Jews and Crusaders (in Arabic, Al Qaeda, or the base) announced their mission: "to kill Americans and their allies, both civil and military, is an individual duty of every Muslim who is able, in any country where this is possible." [*SCS*, 1/14/01] One may wonder what happened to this youngest of twenty-four brothers (his father has some 52 children) in his childhood, despite all the family money and the education they all received, to produce this monster.

Bin Laden's reach, using his thousands of fanatical veterans, has extended throughout the world. The camps in Afghanistan trained members in the use of weapons, explosives, kidnapping, urban fighting, counterintelligence, and even chemical and biological warfare.

His trainees also received instruction from Hezbollah (the Iranian Shiite group in Lebanon), who were experts in making car bombs. There seemed to be no conflict between their medieval social agenda and their fondness for CD-ROMs and the latest technologies for mayhem.

Fortunately for the world, this movement has a built-in time bomb: corruption. These guerrilla groups are financing their activities through kidnapping, which endears them to nobody, and worse— through a vast new network of drug trafficking, most of the materials coming from Afghanistan and Pakistan. Moderate Muslims complain that Islam thus receives an unfair black eye from these thoroughly evil adherents.

Drug trafficking has become one of the most lucrative criminal activities in Russia, and Russia's addicts may number over three million. Central Asia's heroin reaches countries in the west, too.

It appears that "the enemy of my enemy" is not always my friend. The United States never should have supported the Afghan "Freedom Fighters" against the Russians. However, this error was remedied when the US invaded Afghanistan, drove out the Taliban and Osama, and has been trying to reconstruct the country to make it once more viable. An astonishing election was held that gave Afghans some hope for the future. It is just a beginning.

Sudan

Sudan has a sad history as a backwater of belligerent conservatism. This largest country in Africa borders on Egypt, the Red Sea, Eritrea, Ethiopia, Kenya, Uganda, Congo, Central African Republic, Chad, and Libya. Most of these countries are listed high in the catalogs of disasters, but Sudan tops the list.

The country is divided among three main groups: the northerners, mostly Arab; the westerners, Muslims who immigrated from West Africa; and the southerners, Nilotic and Sudanese people, mostly Black, who are Animists or Christian. The rulers in the Arab north are not willing to live and let live.

Sudan was conquered by Egypt in 1823, lured there by a lucrative trade in ivory and slaves. By the late 1870s, the Egyptians were beginning to think twice about the slave trade and determined to end it. This effort led to a Sudanese revolt against Egypt and the establishment of a theocracy in 1881 by a fanatic who assumed the title of al-Mahdi (a reincarnated "hidden" imam). In 1885, there was an infamous battle in which British General Gordon (head of an Anglo-Egyptian force) was defeated.

Egypt gave up on the Sudan, but the British did not. Between 1896–8, the British took control of the Sudan and destroyed the power of the Mahdists. After World War I, Egypt and the Sudan came under British mandate and the elite of both countries were exposed to British education and law.

After World War II, during the period of decolonization, Sudan opted for independence from Egypt, which they received in 1956. The southern Sudanese, however, had justifiable fear that the new nation would be dominated by the Arab Muslim north, and they began a revolt that lasted for seventeen years.

Sudan's existence as a parliamentary republic was ended after only two years by a military coup. The new military government had no success in either improving the country's terrible economy or ending the civil war, so it returned the country to civilian rule.

The civilians did no better. In 1969, there was another coup, and the new dictator, Col. Muhammad Gaafur al-Nimeiry, banned all political parties, nationalized banks and industries, and ended the civil war by granting southern Sudan some autonomy, on which he later reneged.

Political instability increased throughout the country, and in 1983 Nimeiry, to court the support of the masses, instituted strict Islamic law for the country. The horrors of this move for modern, educated Sudanese, particularly for women, cannot be overestimated. But, to make matters even worse, the government nullified its agreement with the south and declared war, a war that continues to this day.

Whatever development the country could have enjoyed since then has gone away. After nearly two decades of unremitting warfare, whole regions of the country have abandoned what subsistence agriculture they had and famine is endemic.

The war has cost more lives from conflict and resultant famine than the slaughters in Kosovo, Bosnia, Rwanda, and Somalia combined—an estimated two million. [*SFC*, 1/7/01]

In one region alone, Nuba, the population was reduced from 1.3 million in 1985 to 250,000 now. This can be counted as genocide.

The issue here is not just religion; it is also an interesting manifestation of Arab cultural imperialism, an issue not much discussed until brought up by V.S. Naipal's most recent book, *Beyond Belief*.

Naipal raises the issue of Arab Muslim conversion of countries that were not Arab: Turkey, Iran, Northern India (Pakistan and Bangladesh), Malaysia, and Indonesia. In all of these countries, there was an effort to blot out all memory of pre-Islamic culture in the category of "jahilia" (the time of ignorance of Islam).

Arab Muslim culture was substituted for the past, which has created what Naipal sees as a certain schizophrenia among these peoples. The Iranians always fought this pressure, to the extent that they adopted a separate sect of Islam, Shi'a, which co-opted many elements of their prior state religion, Zoroastrianism. During the twentieth century, the Pahlavi dynasty took on this issue frontally, and there is still a struggle between Iranian nationalists and Islamic fundamentalists.

Secular Turks have also taken on this issue through their officially secular governance, and there has been a movement to research pre-Islamic Turkish culture.

Pakistanis and Afghans have lost the struggle. The money pouring in to promote Arabic language and Arab Islam is brainwashing the current generation of uneducated young men and boys throughout Central Asia, from Afghanistan through northern Pakistan.

This same campaign has been going on for years in rural Malaysia and Indonesia, and includes scholarships to bring promising students to Saudi Arabia for further study and indoctrination. The fanatics being so indoctrinated are securing leadership positions in rural areas and are threatening and Islamizing their governments.

In Afghanistan's border area with Pakistan, of course, Islamists are ruling with dire results for everyone. Northern Pakistan is coming apart and is virtually ungovernable by the central government.

Yemen

For twenty-one years, Yemen, an exceedingly poor and backward Muslim state, was divided into two countries: the Marxist-controlled South Yemen and the Muslim-controlled North.

Once more, as in Afghanistan, the Cold War forced the West into a position that it would not have taken otherwise: support of religious reactionaries rather than the Soviet-backed modernizers. The results have been devastating for Yemen, with the triumph of the reactionaries upon the reuniting of the two Yemens.

The irony is that progressive Muslim states such as Iran and Egypt joined with the West in supporting the side in this struggle that would later come to unseat the late Shah and is in the process of unseating the semi-secular Egyptian government.

For the twenty-one years that Marxists controlled South Yemen, men and women were equal under the law, and had the same rights to work and be educated. The condition of women in the South was light-years different than those of the North, who lived in total suppression. [*SFC*, 1/19/01]

In South Yemen, before reunification, every person, regardless of gender, went to the Ministry of Labor to get work according to his or her qualifications. Men were not, as today, given automatic preference.

There was free education through college as well as health care and rent control. Women played sports such as basketball and enjoyed athletic clubs. The social benefits were marvelous, but the economy collapsed under the burden. The South could not defend itself against the North, and reintegration really meant surrender to a system that again permits men to marry up to four wives. Wives must obey their husbands and only husbands may seek divorce, a condition that had been addressed by South Yemen's law.

Women are no longer free to move around the muggy seaport town of Aden in clothes reasonable for the climate. They are now compelled to stifle in "Islamic hijab," total black cover-up.

The split in Yemen has interesting historic reverberations: the British ruled Aden and the South, whereas the North was under conservative Ottoman rule. Although Yemen became a republic in 1962, it has never really been unified; conservative tribal and religious figures had more power than the central government, and there was no clear notion of nationhood. The South revolted and became a separate nation, only to lose this status after reunification.

It seems much worse to lose one's freedom than to never have had it at all, which is the case with the next country we will review.

Saudi Arabia

While Saudi Arabia, a theocratic monarchy, has never had a democracy to lose, it had achieved a certain stability and a prominent place in the world due to its oil wealth. There has been enough money around to pacify the public until recently, when the birthrate shot up and ate most of the budget surplus.

The Islamic puritanism that characterizes Saudis' own Wahhabi sect has not only made life in the Kingdom resemble a giant, repressive boys' school, but has also fueled the recent missionary efforts around the rest of the Muslim world, focusing on Muslim states that were modernizing and fairly secular. While this effort is creating mayhem around the world, it also has the potential to come home to bite the Saudi monarchy.

Saudi prosperity has created a population explosion for them that may threaten their future. [*SFC*, 1/7/01] With more than two-fifths of the population under fourteen, the demand for jobs is enormous, and the oil bonanza no longer provides cradle-to-grave largess. Furthermore, the most hated institution among the young is the Religious Police, the Muttawa, which watches all public behavior and administers instant punishment for un-Islamic behavior. Almost anything pleasant seems to them un-Islamic.

Incredible as it seems, the Saudi monarchy is not only under threat from the modernizers, but also on the other side from Islamic factions that want to destroy modern life altogether. Most famous among these is a Saudi of Yemeni extraction, the notorious terrorist Osama bin Laden, currently directing his worldwide network, probably from northern Pakistan.

With sufficient bad luck, Saudi Arabia could revert to the flea-bitten country it once was—hungry and, like Afghanistan, eternally enmeshed in tribal and feudal warfare. [The book to read is *At the Drop of the Veil*, by Marianne Alireza]

Pakistan

The threat to Pakistan's secular status will be described in the next chapter. However, Pakistan should appear in this chapter as well because large parts of the country are already ungovernable by the central administration and have been literally taken over by fundamentalists. It will also appear in the chapter on Twisted Thinking.

Pakistan is disintegrating into a very dangerous anarchy where warlords rule and, when not fighting each other, they are tyrannizing their populations through their own warped notion of Islam.

Political Islam, as interpreted by these warlords, is a dreadful perversion of one of the world's great and potentially humane faiths. Despite the religious fascism practiced by the Islamists, Islam is capable of modernizing and integrating into the secular world.

Reports have come out of Pakistan for the past decade that address the issue of Pakistan's near collapse and resultant chaos. A feature article, "The Sword of Islam" by Tim McGirk [*Time Magazine*, 9/28/98], noted that Pakistan was coming apart at the seams.

When Pakistan was ostracized after its nuclear tests, and on the edge of economic collapse, "Prime Minister Mian Mohammed Nawaz Sharif tried to make the Islamic Republic of Pakistan even more Islamic than it already is." The military has since deposed Sharif, and the authoritarian dictator, Pervez Musharaf, a passionate secularist, is hanging on by a thread. There are limits to what even this bold man can do in a deeply dysfunctional country.

McGirk noted that the country's seventy-two Muslim sects and subsects are at each others' throats, and their long support of Afghanistan's Taliban is coming back to bite them. The struggle over

Kashmir was driving the country to near bankruptcy. "Pakistan may run out of foreign exchange by the end of the month, and the Karachi stock exchange imploded after the May 28 underground nuclear tests, wiping out half its share value." Despite this draconian view, Pakistan is still there.

According to the well-respected Karachi newspaper, *Dawn*, people "just want a little improvement in their lives from the tyranny and callousness of Pakistani officialdom." More Islam will just increase that tyranny. Pakistan will then have a religious dictator, a supreme arbiter of what is considered good and evil under Islam.

Women's associations are protesting. "With this new law, do they want to enter houses to see if someone is offering prayers or not?"

Shiites (15 percent of the population) have had good reason to be worried and Sunni extremists are having a field day. A mullah named Maulana Sufi Mohammed decided to enforce strict Shari'a law in his mountain valley near the Afghan border. "He prohibited driving on the left side of the road because the left hand is deemed unclean. Numerous car crashes failed to deter him." His thugs also destroyed TVs and set up roadblocks to stop cars and rip out music cassettes.

Reports of this sort have filtered out since then, and, of course, a military dictator took over the country in the interim, heroically trying to rescue Pakistan's secular government. The government has been pressured from the outside to hold elections, but observers are not optimistic that Pakistan can manage a democracy.

Two other major articles came out between summer and fall of the year 2000. The earlier was a piece from *The New York Times Magazine*, June 25, 2000: "Inside Jihad U." by Jeffrey Goldberg. See more in Chapter 6, "Twisted Thinking."

The author spent some months risking his neck in what may be one of the most volatile areas in the world. He made the trek to a number of religious "schools," where he found hundreds of little boys being trained to become warriors for this highly specialized sort of Islam. In one Pakistani religious school, the Haqqania Madrasa, Osama bin Laden is a hero, the Taliban's leaders are famous alumni, and the next generation of mujahedeen is being militantly groomed.

"When they got used to me," Goldberg said, "most of the students expressed interest in talking about sex. I was asked whether American men were allowed by law to keep boyfriends and girlfriends at the same time."

In summary, he concludes, "These are poor and impressionable boys kept entirely ignorant of the world and, for that matter, largely ignorant of all but one interpretation of Islam. They are the perfect jihad machines."

In another article, "The Lawless Frontier," by Robert Kaplan [*The Atlantic Monthly*, 9/2000], this peripatetic journalist spent some months exploring the tribal lands of the Afghan-Pakistan border, believing that events there reveal the future of conflict in the Indian subcontinent, along with the dark side of globalization.

Kaplan toured Baluchistan, a western province of Pakistan that is awash in murders, kidnapping, and a revolutionary Pashtoon National People's Party who want an independent "Pashtoonistan." "The government wants to destroy the tribal system, but there are no institutions to replace it," said one tribal chief. "The tribes are large social-welfare networks." (They support themselves by drug smuggling and, lately, kidnapping.)

Pakistan in fact, could be a Yugoslavia in the making, said Kaplan, but with nuclear weapons. Globalization is not a uniform coat of paint. It can lead to war and chaos as easily as to prosperity and human rights. Popular fascination with Afghanistan, Osama bin Laden, and the fighting in Kashmir obscures what Kaplan sees as the core issue of South Asia: the institutional meltdown of Pakistan.

"My comparison to 1980s Yugoslavia, a place that I also saw first-hand, is not casual. In both cases it was the very accumulation of disorder and irrationality that was so striking and that must be described in detail, not merely stated, to be understood."

Kaplan states that the Taliban embody a lethal combination: "a primitive tribal creed, a fierce religious ideology, and the sheer incompetence, naiveté, and cruelty that are begot by isolation."

He further observes a phenomenon familiar to all observers of the Third World: conspiracy theories. These theories of grandiose conspiracies being responsible for their miserable plight (perpetrators are the US and Israel today; they used to be Great Britain and the Russians in the past) are inflamed by illiteracy. People who cannot read rely on hearsay. In Pakistan the adult literacy rate is below 33 percent. In the tribal areas it is below that. "As for the percentage of women in Parachinar who can read, I heard figures as low as two percent; nobody really knows," says Kaplan.

In visiting a number of religious schools (madrasas), Kaplan, like Goldberg, noted that there was no real learning there. These schools were just training camps for future killers.

One educated Pakistani confessed to Kaplan that he had read "The Federalist Papers" and Mill's "On Liberty." "Every single ingredient they say is required for a civil society—you name it, we haven't got it."

There should be plenty of concern on the part of nuclear disarmament organizations that the feebler the state becomes, the more that nuclear weapons are needed to prove its manhood.

One piece of nonsense to come out of Pakistan was the arrest of a professor, Dr. Younus Shaikh, an MD teaching at a medical college. Blasphemy is now a capital crime in Pakistan, and the lynch mobs are eager to enforce this law against the hapless professor, who was asked, in a physiology class, about seventh-century Arabia and its practices regarding circumcision and the removal of underarm hair. All the doctor said was that before the advent of Islam, these two Muslim practices were not part of Arabia's culture. The students were outraged because of the implication that the Prophet Mohammad himself was not circumcised nor armpit shaved. This was taken by the fanatics as blasphemy against the Prophet. [*NY Times*, 5/12/01]

Central Asia

The chaos in northern Pakistan is erupting into the other Muslim states in Central Asia that were formerly part of the Soviet Union. The Russians are alarmed by this and are taking steps to contain the danger. Russian military forces are lined up on Tajikistan's border, keeping the peace, they say. Tajikistan's secular government barely survived a rebellion fomented by Shiite Islamists; the Russians want to keep it that way.

There were reports from Uzbekistan that a serious secret war was being waged in this nation of twenty-four million against pious Muslims by the government. Human rights advocates noted that religious leaders, 4000 to 5000 Muslim men, have been imprisoned with systematic torture, from beatings to extraction of toenails, resulting in some deaths. Government officials deny using torture, but justify other harsh steps on the grounds of saving their country from turning into another Iran or, even worse, Afghanistan. Central Asia can be called a "rough neighborhood" indeed, but the stakes are high for a country that wants to thrive at all. [*SFC*, 11/3/00]

Nigeria

Nigeria will be discussed in Chapter 3, countries with secular governments that are under siege. It appears in this chapter, however, because the northern parts of Nigeria have virtually discarded secular law in favor of their interpretation of Islamic law, and the central government is doing nothing about this. Thus we can explore this region to see how religious fascism looks in Nigeria and what may be its consequences.

Nigeria, like so many countries in Africa, is a recently formed country, and the national borders have more to do with former colonial decisions than with reality. Nigeria is made up of a number of ethnic groups, some of them with low literacy, which makes identification with the nation problematical.

Complicating ethnicity further is religion. The northern half of the country has remained the most backward and conservative and is, in addition, staunchly Muslim. The south is the more developed area and is largely Christian. However, Christian minorities do live in the north, and Muslim minorities in the south, and the tension is rising.

With the implementation of Islamic law in the north, the Christian minorities feel persecuted, which they are. In the south, Muslim minorities are asserting themselves and want Islamic law rather than secular law to govern them.

The government is showing remarkable restraint, considering that the constitution guarantees secular law as national law and this should prevail over Sharia. No one is making this happen, however, and there is a good possibility that Nigeria could find itself, as one scholar notes, an Islamic Republic of Nigeria. [*Nigeria World Publications*, 10/23/99, Ed. Dr. Femi Ajayi]

A scandalous demonstration of Sharia law has received international attention. Muhammud Tukur Anka, the judge in the Nigerian state Zamfara, which has enforced Muslim law, sentenced a seventeen-year-old girl to 180 lashes for engaging in premarital sex. He chose not to believe her testimony that three middle-aged men from her village pressured her into sex and that her own father pressured her into having sex, the money to go to him, presumably. [*CSM*, 1/3/01]

The sentence was carried out forty days after she gave birth, despite protests from around the world. The governor revoked the 80 lashes for "false accusation," but the 100 were administered to the frail girl.

The governor of Zamfara did not expect the federal government to revoke the sentence, but even if it did, the governor planned to ignore it. He considered Islamic law to trump secular law. Furthermore, Anka shrugged off the foreign allegations of human rights abuses. "We don't mind about human rights. We are following the rule of Allah," he said. "Therefore we don't care whatever the people are saying." [*SFC*, 1/23/01]

However, the world did not let it go. In an unusual move for a foreign government official, the Canadian Foreign Minister John Manley said he was worried by what he called the "appalling case." He told the press that the Canadian government had made a number of interventions with the Nigerian government, asking them to respect their own commitments and the UN's Universal Declaration of Human Rights, three amendments of which would be violated by this action. [Reuters, 1/9/01]

"The cloak of religious law cannot be used to justify a sentence like flogging a teenager to death...Those who would tolerate or condone the flogging of Ms. Magazu must hear the roar of outrage from the world." [*The Vancouver Sun*, 1/8/01]

Nigeria is facing not only international condemnation, but is also facing increasing violence between and among religious factions. The Christians living in the Muslim north are not happy under Sharia law that has banned alcohol, closed down cinemas, driven away prostitutes, and segregates the sexes at school and on buses. The fanatics are pressing everyone who can do so to grow a beard.

Indeed, Nigeria is beset by many social ills, starting with the pervasive corruption from top government officials down, and it suffers from the social ills that derive from population explosion and the exodus of so many rural people to urban areas.

In their understandable desire to address the malaise, playing the Sharia card is so draconian that it may kill the host. Since Zamfara state embraced Sharia, a neighboring state, Kaduna, was considering a similar move. This resulted in hundreds of deaths when Christians and Muslims took to the streets in conflict. [*CSM*, 5/26/00]

A new twist on Sharia jurisprudence in Zamfara is the rise of "monitoring committees" with the power to arrest Muslim criminals. These are, of course, vigilante groups, religious thugs who mete out on-the-spot beatings to suspected lawbreakers. They look for people using alcohol, prostitutes, gamblers, and co-ed public transportation. A new highway sign as one enters Zamfara state reads: "Welcome to Zamfara, Home of Farming and Sharia." Indeed. [*SFC*, 1/23/01]

Looking at the chaos in Nigeria as an historian, the only justification that I can see in this religious polarization is that perhaps this is one way of moving people from tribal identification to something larger. Nigeria, like many relatively new countries, has great difficulty in inspiring people to move from tribal to national identity. The educated elite does better than the uneducated masses in this.

Even a country as relatively homogeneous as modern Turkey had this problem when Kamal Ataturk forcibly modernized the country in the 1920s and 30s. He used education and a national military to move the people from village and tribal affiliations to national.

However, using the religion card for this purpose may be putting a more optimistic spin on this phenomenon than warranted. It is clearly dangerous, both to the aim of national identity and to religion itself.

Who are the leaders of religious fascist movements? Do they have Western educations, and if so, why is critical thinking so lacking in both the leadership and the followers? Chapter 4 will discuss these questions.

We have just enough religion to make us hate, but not enough to make us love one another.
　　　　　　　—Jonathan Swift, 1667–1745

Chapter 3.
Challenges to secular states

Early in the 1990s, when the military government of Algeria held their first real election in that country, the preliminary votes in many municipalities looked as if Muslim Fundamentalists were winning. The government quickly canceled the elections, and howls of condemnation came from democracies the world over.

In theory, if one believes in democracy, the results should determine the next government, no matter how disagreeable to one faction or another. However, the theory does not take into consideration an election in which one side believes in "one man, one vote, one time." This was the case in Germany in 1933, when Hitler won by a plurality (not a majority); after he took office, there were no more elections.

The Islamists in Algeria posed a similar threat, and the secular military government reacted with force. Were they wrong? Although many people voted for the Islamic parties only because the corrupt military government had not provided any other alternatives in their heavy-handed rule, these voters did not consider the consequences. As bad as the military government was, there was much more freedom for people to live their lives as they saw fit (a secular value) than if the Islamists had taken over. If one doubts this, Iran and Afghanistan offer graphic examples of what loss of freedom means.

This is not to justify the heavy hand of a military government, but it is to have a closer look at the alternative. Turkey is another secular country that is being challenged by Islamists, and the government is standing firm and enjoys the support of the secular and non-political military in defending the secular nature of Turkey's government. This earns them the opprobrium of human rights advocates in Europe who do not seem to comprehend what is at stake here.

It is essential to understand that secular societies, under secular rule, believe in minimal interference in private life. In Iran, where I spent much time between 1957 and 1979, the year of the Islamic takeover, I witnessed a society in which the pious could cover up their women in chadors and where members of the secular community could wear—and do—what they pleased.

The press was not free to criticize the Shah, and professors in the universities were not free to lead student revolts. However, Iranians did not hesitate to speak their minds among themselves, and indeed they did. Nobody in the government engaged in mind control. Nobody grilled elementary school students to find out what their parents thought and said at home. And there was a general atmosphere of live and let live in a public that ran the gamut from peasants, workers, migratory tribes, and city people to an elite that was open to change.

With the takeover of the Islamic Fundamentalist revolution under the late Ayatollah Khomeini, live and let live died. The dress code, particularly for women, was enforced with rigor. The schools devote half of their time to religious instruction, a system that involves memorization and no questioning. Obedience is the major quality desired in students and the general public as well. And if people did not want their homes invaded, they were wise to leave their window curtains open so that the religious police could see that nothing "un-Islamic" was going on.

The other model of Islam gone amok was Afghanistan, a nightmare world any way one looks at it, which will be addressed in the next chapter. It is truly a cautionary tale. Although the Taliban no longer rules, the repressions of Islamism still prevail outside of the biggest cities.

The countries in this chapter are surveyed roughly west to east.

Algeria

Let us return to Algeria. After the military canceled the election, the Islamists fought back. Fierce battles took place between Islamic rebel factions and the government, which prevailed in urban areas.

At that point, the factions went underground with a terror campaign in the cities to intimidate women into adopting Islamic covering. A number of women at a favorite beach were found decapitated for having the effrontery of wearing swimsuits. Professional women were harassed, some assassinated, and there were some acid attacks on unveiled university students.

In the countryside, things were even worse. These Islamic sects became night riders, attacking villages, murdering whole households, and kidnapping young women to serve as sex slaves. This still goes on sporadically.

Elections have been held since this horror was unleashed, and the Islamists have lost handily. The voters finally realized what was at stake.

The Islamists are using a very warped interpretation of this religion for their own purposes, which appear to be seizure of political control and a revolt against modern human rights values. A key element of this revolt has to do with women, which will be addressed in a later chapter of this book.

As a matter of fact, Jewish ultra-Orthodoxy in Israel and Hindu ultra-orthodoxy in India have also used their versions of religion to rebel against the same social changes that characterize modern secular life. There are just more cases of Muslims playing this role around the world than Jews or Hindus—or, for that matter, certain Buddhists—but they all represent a threat to secular societies.

Egypt

Egypt, with a stable military government, has had serious brushes with fundamentalists. Members of one such group assassinated President Sadat, but their attempt at takeover did not succeed. Since then, there have been attacks on tourists, including a massacre at a favorite tourist site. This did manage to damage the tourism industry to this day. This was an attack on a very important source of national income, which was its intent.

On a much quieter level, there has been a movement among women to adopt Islamic dress and head covering. Some of this, as in Iran before the revolution, is motivated by symbolic rebellion against the government. While some of this movement represents genuine new piety on the part of women, much of it is the fruit of intimidation. Several university women who did not cover up had acid thrown in their faces by men who objected to their immodesty. The book to read about this is *The Nine Parts of Desire*, by Geraldine Brooks. Brooks was astonished to see her very emancipated secretary succumb to Islamist pressures to retreat to hijab and an arranged marriage.

Recently, a student at the elite American University in Cairo attempted to go to class in a full black veil, covering even her eyes. This presents a problem that goes beyond freedom of choice; security becomes an issue. How can one check the identity of a completely cloaked person? Who is to say it is not a terrorist? And how does a proctor check identity at an exam? Freedom from religion is being eroded in great chunks in Egypt day by day. [*CSM*, 1/17/01]

To women of an older generation who reveled in their emancipation from traditional Islam, it is grievous to see their own daughters giving up their freedom for what seems a half-baked political statement or intimidation.

The latest descent of Egypt into Islamicism has been played out in the courts: censorship of novels, one trial to enforce divorce of a woman writer from her husband of nearly 50 years on grounds of apostasy (happily the judge threw it out of court), and a show trial of homosexuals. All of these cases bode ill for secular rule.

Nigeria

Nigeria, a former British colony that showed great promise of success, considering its potential natural wealth, including petroleum, is instead a disaster.

One of the most corrupt governments in the world has held control, and despite recent respectable elections, general corruption is not going away.

Education has been neglected, along with an improvement of the low status of women, and the result is a raging population explosion and ethnic hostilities that have flared to major civil war in the past.

The northern region of Nigeria is heavily Muslim, and religious fascism has taken over, to the point of replacing secular (British) law with Sharia law. This movement stymies a new reform government from doing something about Nigeria's chaos.

Nigeria has problems in common with many Third World countries: an enormous gap between the educated elite and the masses of the ignorant, who are still mired in tribal religions or political Islam. The flight of poor villagers to the cities has exacerbated Nigeria's problems. AIDS is rampant, with adults of working age dying in large numbers, making economic problems even more serious.

Worst of all is the disparity between the oil wealth rolling in and how little of it has reached the people who need it. Political Islamists will not make this better, unless they go after corruption with as much zeal as they go after women's sexual offenses. See Chapter 2 for an exploration of life under political Islam in the north.

Turkey

Turkey has been fighting the battle for a secular state since Kamal Ataturk emerged as the father of modern Turkey, right after World War I. Because of his prestige as a military hero in the war and as the savior of what was left of the Ottoman Empire, the Turkish homeland, his social revolution met minimal opposition. For several decades, he diligently attempted to establish those new institutions for Turkey that obviously had played such an important role in the development of modern Europe and America.

He developed a modern army that was to remain resolutely non-political and resolutely secular. He supported public education, emancipation of women and men from what he considered oppressive religious conformity, and he tirelessly visited villages in an attempt to begin grassroots democracy.

Over the past half-century, Turkey has had several close calls with anarchy, and each time the military stepped in to reestablish civic peace and then returned the country to civilian rule.

The challenge now is coming from the eastern half of the country, a region that has not yet shared in the prosperity of the secular west. It is a region lacking water, underdeveloped and poor, and, in the grip of traditional religion, it has suffered a population explosion.

Every city of any size in Turkey is surrounded by villages of squatters from eastern Turkey, and Islamists have rushed in to win the hearts and minds of these potential subjects. This is creating internal stress for the country.

The government's position is that no government institution will permit female Islamic headscarves because that would imply government support of religion. Women may wear anything they please on the street or in a private enterprise, but not in Parliament, government offices, or the state universities.

The latest challenge to secular rule involved the Minister of Health, who, motivated by personal religious zeal, demanded virginity tests for nursing students in government-sponsored schools. After an outraged response from women and civil libertarians, the Prime Minister ordered the Minister of Health to take a vacation immediately.

The Turkish government, unlike the Egyptian, will not knuckle under to this camel's nose under the tent. Turkey knows what will happen if the Islamists take over. They live next door to Iran.

Pakistan

It would be difficult to imagine any changes more destructive to Pakistan's future existence than the transformation of religious Islam into political Islam.

This country was created some fifty years ago after the withdrawal of Great Britain from colonial occupation of the Indian subcontinent. Out of fear that liberation of India would disadvantage Muslim Indians, the subcontinent was divided between India and much smaller Pakistan, a country divided into two distant sectors, east and west.

The very idea of Pakistan was similar to that of Israel: a refuge for both secular and religious co-religionists. Today, this country is no refuge for secular Indian Muslims, who have lost much of their freedom to political Islam, nor is it even a refuge for religious Muslims, who are going after each other's sectarian difference with murderous zeal.

One cannot necessarily blame Islam as a religion for this state of affairs. Islam entered India as a breath of fresh air with its egalitarianism and lack of caste. However, over time, Indian Muslims and Indian Hindus have given their worst cultural elements to each other and have shared none of the better religious insights. The Indian Muslims who are now Pakistanis have unofficially embraced caste, an institution that would have horrified the Prophet Mohammad, who was resolutely egalitarian. And in India a movement of Hindu fundamentalism and nationalist Hinduism assumes the worst aspect of political Islam: murderous fanaticism. Both ideologies suppress women and dislike literacy for the masses. Both are innately anti-democratic.

India's fabled tolerance has floundered, and it is only the modern sector, which is now flourishing in the south, which keeps that value alive.

Pakistan in the course of its 50-some years of statehood has not fostered literacy (its female literacy is one of the worst in the world—barely 5 percent). Without literacy, the economy remains backward, population explosion destabilizes and impoverishes further, and the gap between the educated and uneducated assumes Grand Canyon proportions.

The sort of Islam that was adopted and institutionalized in this once secular state has been a disaster. Former dictator Zia did not enjoy caste and family status to back him up, so he chose instead Pakistan's own peculiar Islam to appeal to the most ignorant masses. What pleased his constituents was repealing elements of modern secular law (of British origin) and replacing them with benighted Islamic law, directed at the suppression of women (the so-called Zena laws), a Pakistani specialty. The poor downtrodden men at the bottom of the caste heap were gratified to have someone lower to kick.

Democracy in Pakistan is really not a possibility with the level of illiteracy and ignorance that is there today. Voting is a matter of purchasing votes, scarcely a democratic system.

Fundamentalists are flexing their muscles and have been putting pressure on a government that is obviously in flux. Although many Pakistanis are secular, they do not have a platform.

In the Afghan-dominated refugee centers, such as Peshwar, the religious fascists have shut down cable TV operations and music halls. Banners recently appeared across the city calling for restoration of the caliphate.

The effects of radical Islam have reached the rest of the country too.

Professors are noting that in the past most female students were unveiled, but few dare come unveiled today.

In a recent incident, Muslim clerics protested a new program that allows women to be public bus drivers. They claim that allowing women to work is immoral. "Islam gives full freedom to women, but only within four walls." [*SFC*, 12/25/01]

A courageous secular General, Pervez Musharraf, seized power from a "civilian government" (a kind description) in a bloodless coup in October, 1999. Under great pressure by the uncomprehending democrats in the Western world, he was laboring to ready the country for federal elections at the end of 2002 with municipal and district council elections to begin sooner. [*SFC*, 12/31/00]

In a bid for a more egalitarian democracy, he planned to allocate one-third of the seats for women and one-third for the poor. His heart was in the right place, but he was in the wrong country.

The Islamist attacks on 9/11 have changed all these plans. Nobody is pressing Musharraf to push for elections now. They know how they would come out.

During Musharraf's attempts at preparing for elections, some serious obstacles emerged. Women were reluctant to run because of threats from their husbands. One woman was reportedly killed by her husband for refusing to withdraw her candidacy. The few women who planned to run may have been tools of landlords who would control their votes.

There is no way to campaign in a country of illiterates when a woman's picture cannot be displayed and where public meetings cannot be held with women present.

Pakistan is hoisted on its own petard, which is a shame, because fifty years ago there was hope, and had the country been resolutely secular and had it done what nation builders must do—break with the worst aspects of the past—they would be well on the way to modern state status today.

One must not be deluded into thinking that just because Pakistan has nuclear technology that it can sustain it. The schools that are available today for boys (girls are not welcome) are Islamic madrasas, financed by Saudi money, and they teach poor boys to memorize the Koran in a language foreign to them. [Kaplan and Goldberg]

The graduates of such places appear willing to lob nuclear weapons on their imagined enemies (Israel and the US), but none of them will ever learn to think, nor will they get into a university to become tomorrow's nuclear engineers.

Bangladesh

What started out fifty years ago as East Pakistan was the result of geography. The most concentrated Muslim regions of India were in the northwest and northeast corners, and these became East and West Pakistan. They had nothing more in common than Islam. The secular educated members of both regions spoke English and had Western education in common. But among the mass lower level, not even the languages were the same.

West Pakistan dominated the new country and it did not take very long for the East to know they were in the grip of West Pakistani corruption and power. The West had military clout while the East had the flower of Indian Muslim (Bengali) culture—writers and poets. It was no contest.

With the help of India, East Pakistan fought for its independence from West Pakistan and renamed itself Bangladesh, in honor of its Bengali origins.

Its freedom notwithstanding, Bangladesh is not a happy place either, and fundamentalist Islam is playing as devastating a role there as in today's Pakistan. The educated and secular are constantly under siege by fanatics. Women are suffering from a new curse: acid attacks on their faces by rebuffed suitors or just by men who think they are "too proud." [SFC, 11/17/00]

The poverty that accompanies countries with low literacy, low status for women, and reactionary religious and social systems (caste), dogs Bangladesh as it does Pakistan and northern India. The entire region's population explosion, including the neighboring mountain states where river headwaters are, has denuded the forests and floodwaters are pouring down into the Bangladeshi deltas. The floods have been accompanied by rising ocean waters, possibly because of global warming, and it appears that within half a century Bangladesh may indeed be under water. Where will the desperate population go?

The one good thing that has come out of that unfortunate land has been a Western-educated economist, Grameen, who began a revolutionary project some 20 years ago. He prevailed upon his bank to start making small loans to women to start small businesses. The women form cooperative circles to guarantee each others' loans, and the success rate of this venture has been remarkable. Many women have been lifted out of poverty by such simple business ventures as buying a cell phone and charging a small fee to users in their community. The country does not have telephone service—or any other services, for that matter—in rural regions.

Craft workshops and other mini-businesses are offering the first hope these people have had, and the idea has been replicated in areas as far away as Africa and even in the poverty belt of the United States, the Appalachian backwoods.

Bangladesh does not need more Islam, more poverty, and more population. Yet that is all that is offered by the reactionaries who still fight the secular world.

India

India shares some characteristics with Pakistan, but, fortunately, there is more hope for a better outcome. India enjoys a remarkable number of university graduates, many of them good enough to make Indian engineers and computer technologists welcome to work around the world—and now, the work comes to them.

What India has not had enough of, over its fifty-odd years of independence, is equal development. There are parts of India in which there are no grade schools (although the convoluted government bureaucracy thinks there are), where the caste system is alive and well, and where life for a woman is sheer hell.

This misery and ignorance has produced an alarming population explosion (the one-billionth Indian baby was born in 1999), ecological degradation from a watershed poisoned by the very chemicals that made the Green Revolution possible, and a new crisis in the countryside: the revolt of the Untouchables, formerly the passive slaves of the castes above them. In one recent case, a landlord and hired thugs invaded an Untouchable village and slaughtered the women and children in their beds. [SF Examiner, 618/01]

India calls itself "the world's largest democracy," and it can make that claim on numbers. However, the quality of that democracy can be questioned since the 50 percent illiteracy rate makes for the same corruption problems of vote-buying that Pakistan has.

This sort of illiterate democracy has given rise to Hindu nationalism: a political cult that calls for a return to all the worst aspects of Hinduism, the abandonment of English for local languages, and the reaffirmation of the horrific status of women. A few years ago, Hindu fundamentalists took on the popular import of Valentine's Day in a rampage of torching card shops and burning Valentine cards. They see threats to their values everywhere, it seems. [National Public Radio, 2/14/01]

Happily, however, these fanatics lost the last election. This a good sign.

Where hope enters in is the emergence of an educated sector in the south of India, which has spawned a science and technology boom having an effect around the world. Secular Indians are very proud of this, and the growth of an enormous middle class is encouraging.

Indian genius in antiquity gave the world the concept "zero," which revolutionized math. Their descendants today demonstrate math genius still.

One interesting fruit of Indian democracy, as flawed as it is, is that an Untouchable became head of state a few years ago and many other Untouchables are securing educations and showing themselves to be competent and intelligent indeed.

The great Mahatma Gandhi tried to tell his countrymen this truth half a century ago. They were not ready to listen.

Malaysia

The former British colony of Malaya was broken up into two countries upon independence: the Muslim state of Malaysia and the secular city-state of Singapore. The differences between the two states are very revealing.

Singapore is a multi-ethnic city-state comprised of Chinese, Malay, and Indian citizens, but dominated by the Chinese. The country has been run by a most amazing personality, Lee Kwan Yu, who could well qualify for Aristotle's notion of a Philosopher King. He shaped this country from a decayed backwater fifty years ago into one of the most developed and well run countries in today's world. The brainpower of governance is resolutely Chinese and secular. Rigid birth control and universal education has produced a stable population with one of the highest standards of living in Asia and the fruits of this bounty are universal for Singaporeans of all ethnicities.

Malaysia, a much larger country with a dominant Malay population and a small Chinese elite had every economic advantage to qualify for membership in ASEAN (the Association of Southeast Asian Nations) and is one of the flourishing states known as the Asian Tigers. But something is happening in Malaysia that is spelling the end of good times and the beginnings of real trouble.

Fundamentalist Islam has been buying power (with Saudi money) in an attempt to end secular rule in that country. [Naipal, *Beyond Belief* and *Among the Believers*] In rural areas, where poverty still prevails, Islamization has taken over. Islamic schools have been set up and financed by Saudi money; promising students are given scholarships to study fundamentalist Islam in Saudi Arabia; and local councils have begun to close nightclubs, re-veil the women, and stir up ethnic hatreds toward Chinese and Indian Christians and Hindus. [Naipal, both books]

The latest folly is to demand that couples walking together must show marriage identification cards if challenged. Failure to do so can get jail terms, beatings, and worse. [*SFC*, 1/2999]

The scenario of all this will be easy to predict: a population explosion, degradation of secular Islam (where it exists at all), and a general impoverishment and growing ethnic stress in the country.

Indonesia

This three-thousand-mile-long country made up of islands is the largest Muslim country in the world. It was the last region to be Islamized, a process introduced by Arab and Muslim Indian traders in the fifteenth century. Indonesia is now almost completely Islamic, except for Bali, which retains its ancient Hindu-Buddhist religion, and a few former Portuguese-colonized islands in which the natives were converted to Catholicism, and a Chinese merchant community that is generally Christian.

While Indonesia remained a secular dictatorship, which it had been since its independence from the Dutch after World War II, sectarian hostilities were kept minimal, emerging only when the government needed a scapegoat for its own financial incompetence. The Chinese have always been the scapegoat of choice. (The one major horror was the slaughter of several million "communists," mostly progressive Chinese, in the 1960s.)

Although it started slowly, the government did finally attempt general public secular education, which, along with a great oil boom, gave rise to an educated, respectable, and large middle class. Out of this middle class came the predictable desire for having more say in their governance. The dictatorship was challenged, and a financial crash spurred by gargantuan corruption finally unseated Dictator Suharto and his family.

Bringing down a dictatorship should be good news, but when coupled with financial stress, all the hidden sectarian hostilities flare up. The Chinese once more took the brunt of this abuse, and many Chinese left Indonesia, taking with them skills that the country badly needs.

In the more remote areas of the country, a campaign of Islamization, again, financed by Saudi money, has had the same effect as that in Malaysia. The hinterlands are going fundamentalist, and with it secular life is being overrun, women are being re-veiled, and ethnic hostilities are flaring. [Naipal, both books]

On Christmas Eve of 2000, there was an organized campaign of bombing Christian churches. [SFC, 12/25/00] Five Catholic and Protestant churches were targeted for bombing in Jakarta, and they appear to have been targets of both Muslims on Christians and Indonesians on their Chinese minority.

The government (in 2001) suspected this was part of an attempt to discredit the current democratically elected government, but the bombings followed a pattern of attacks on Christians in such places as East Timor, which had won independence in late 1999 (despite a pogrom launched by paramilitaries who refused to see Indonesia dismantled).

Another island with a majority Christian population, Aceh, became a battleground between seekers of independence and the hard line military. [*CSM*, 1/19/01]

But despite these setbacks, the 2004 election was the best and most uncorrupt to date. The government seems willing to take on the most murderous of Islamicists and is beginning to turn it around.

The Philippines

The Philippine Islands, once the colonial territory of the United States, was the first colony to receive its independence without struggle from its former master after World War II. This country, unlike its fellow former colonies in the Pacific Rim, failed to thrive for a long time.

Once a colony of Spain, public education was not even considered until the United States took over the country in the Spanish-American War. Development was further hampered by a Catholicism that remained much more like that of Spain in the sixteenth century than the modern Catholic Church with Protestant competition.

To the surprise of formerly hopeless onlookers, the Philippines began to climb out of its hole just fifteen years ago. A flourishing middle class with Western, secular education began to turn this unevenly developed archipelago into a modern state. Their long-time dictator, Marcos, was unseated and democratic elections—flawed but democratic—replaced one-family rule.

The major problem for this country is still its population explosion, a fruit of improved health and a resolutely anti-contraception religion.

Only one region of the Philippines is Muslim—the poorest and southern-most island of Mindanao. It has endured even more neglect from Manila than the other backwaters of the Philippines.

An opportunity presented itself to a sect of fundamentalist and violent Muslims with connections to Osama bin Laden and Afghan terrorists who have set up a lucrative kidnapping business and have been terrorizing Manila with bombings of buses, train depots, and market-places. Attacks during Christmas of 2000 killed 22 people and injured

120. These bombings were aimed at producing as much mayhem as possible among the civilian population. [*SFC*, 1/9/01]

Horrible as this was, there is little likelihood that Fundamentalist Islam will prevail over what is now a secular Philippines. All it can do is to add one more list of crimes to the growing roll from other Muslim fundamentalist groups—and to make life even poorer and more miserable for Philippine Muslims.

South Africa

In the hard-won multi-racial democracy of once authoritarian South Africa, nobody anticipated that there might be a Muslim problem brewing.

Dampening the euphoria of its new democracy has been a crime wave of monumental proportions, juiced by international illegal drugs and an epidemic of rape. Scholars of democracy could tell you that a country with such uneven development as South Africa would have problems with instant, all-inclusive democracy.

Capetown, a lovely city famous for its peaceful multiracialism, has been transformed by Muslim vigilantism. A large number of the colored (mixed blood) citizens who have of late been converted to Islam have taken it upon themselves to clean up the crime wave in Capetown. The community was initially delighted to see drug dealers dragged out and dealt with summarily. Then the vigilantes went after other "criminals," and, before long, were establishing and trying to enforce a nasty social agenda. The most recent action—that finally got the South African government into play—was the firebombing of a nightclub.

The South African government has identified this Muslim group as terrorists—and this is probably not a moment too soon. [National Public Radio, 1/2/01]

Israel

Some fifty years ago, Israel became a state and was admitted to the United Nations. The almost successful Nazi program of exterminating Europe's Jews during World War II gave rise to the need for survivors to have somewhere to go other than their former homes. Since the early twentieth century, a handful of European secular Jews had returned to what they considered their ancient homeland and began preparing it to become a refuge for Jews from all over the world. Israel was to be a country dedicated to Jews of all sorts, from the most religiously indifferent to religious zealots.

The new country was dominated by a European-educated and culturally oriented government. The laws of the country were modern and secular. For their minimal cooperation in the establishment of Israeli government, the Orthodox communities—few in number and isolated by choice— received exemption from military service, acquired control over marriage and divorce, and demanded kosher food only in public restaurants and hotels and no flights on the Sabbath for the national airline.

For fifty years there was a more or less live-and-let-live relationship between the secular and ultra-Orthodox communities. Each tried to have nothing to do with the other, outside of the political necessity of serving in the multi-party parliament.

Suddenly, within the last decade, the ultra-Orthodox have come out of their isolation and have declared open warfare. Secular Israelis who would never have said anything bad about a fellow Jew to the outside world are now realizing what a monster has been created. [Armstrong]

The ultra-Orthodox are well on the road to making Jerusalem, that beloved citadel of three religions, impossible for secular living. Women dressed in normal, modern hot weather clothing are stoned and spat at and called whores. Automobiles that dare to appear in Orthodox neighborhoods during the Sabbath receive the same treatment. Secular Israelis are furious and are having a hard look at the privileges that have been accorded people who are not harmless anymore but are increasingly fascist.

Former President Ehud Barak, who had been struggling to make peace with the Palestinians (in accord with the wishes of 75 percent of both Israelis and Palestinians, so say polls) found the ultra-Orthodox less than helpful. They have seized the opportunity of trying to extort even more privileges in exchange for their reluctant support of Barak's party in Parliament.

Barak was dealing with two sides of Orthodoxy: those who practice an ultra-observant religiosity, and those who use literal interpretations of the Bible to support an ugly religious nationalism. The latter are the settlers, planted amidst Palestinian communities, who are ready to bring the whole country into war to support their notion of a "greater Israel."

In a moment of anger, President Barak openly explored the possibility of putting a cap on the power of Israel's religious fanatics. [*SFC*, 9/18/00]

Barak suggested taking "religion" off of Israeli ID cards, producing the country's first constitution (avoided for the past 52 years), providing public transportation on the Sabbath to end discrimination against families too poor for cars, and privatizing El Al airline to let it fly on Saturdays. He also urged an end to the Orthodox monopoly over rules for marriage and divorce, introducing Sabbath shopping, and forcing religious schools to include secular civics classes.

His words touched a chord with many secular Israelis and certainly with the overseas Jewish communities of the United States and Western Europe who are beginning to reconsider where their money will go. They would like to see Conservative and Reform Judaism recognized in Israel—something that the ultra-Orthodox have prevented.

Secular Israelis are seriously reconsidering the military exemption for the ultra-Orthodox. They do not buy the notion that prayer is a substitute for military defense. They are also examining the alarming birthrate of these religious communities and the consequences for democratic takeover through sheer numbers some day. An additional concern is the amount of money spent on welfare in these communities because the men do not work (they study the Torah) and the women cannot support their huge families. Resentment is setting in.

Along with this, there is a reexamination of the ultra-nationalists in the beleaguered settlements. This was a bad idea from the beginning, and many Israelis are wondering how many of their young soldiers they are willing to lose to protect those unreasonable outposts.

Israel does not have a constitution that protects the rights of the secular. This was much too volatile an issue when they were hastily creating a new country, but if they do not do so now, they may live to regret it later. Modern democracy requires decision-making by an educated electorate, not by self-appointed spokesmen for God.

Palestine

Although not a state yet at the time of this writing, it is apparent that statehood is eventually inevitable. For the fifty years since the founding of Israel and the flight of many Palestinians into exile, the de facto "government" of this state-to-be was the Palestinian Liberation Organization, a group whose leadership was somewhat educated and secular. There are probably more Palestinians with graduate degrees than any other group of Middle Easterners except for Israelis.

Because the process of negotiating with Israel over statehood was slow and seemingly endless, other factions that urged violence rose to the fore. Along with the violence came political Islam, and the secular nature of the future Palestinian state is in danger.

Among the most educated of the Palestinian Arabs are those who are Christian. Once a part of the leadership of the PLO, these leaders have been sidelined, and threats against all Arab Christians from the new militant Islamists are driving Christian Arabs from the region. There has been an exodus of the very people whom the new state would need.

Saudi Arabia

Although certainly not a secular state, this hitherto stable country is at risk. As solid as Saudi Arabia once looked, being a country where only one variety of Islam is permitted and enforced, it is in serious trouble. This is the case of an Islamic country where there is under-ground opposition from factions (such as Shiites and Osama bin Laden) who want the country to be even stricter. It is difficult to tell if religion is the underlying motive, or if it is merely a screen for people who want to topple the Saudi power structure. The Saudi rulers are now fighting a battle for their lives.

Religion is for some people almost as powerful a need as the need for food and water. Most religions provide comfort and community for their followers and are benign, so long as they do not have the force of compulsion. With compulsion, or the arm of the state, they become monstrous.

As painful as is this survey of countries with secular governments under siege by fundamentalist religion, the plight of the states that lost this battle is worse (see Chapter 2).

So long as man remains free he strives for nothing so incessantly and so painfully as to find someone to worship.
——Fedor Dostoevsky,
The Brothers Karamazov (1879–80)

Chapter 4.
Cults enlisting educated followers

T his chapter is personally very difficult to write because I have always considered education the cure for bad behavior. My assumption has been that once a person goes through the long process of learning the process of critical thinking is the automatic payoff.

Regrettably this is not so. We human beings have an amazing capacity to compartmentalize knowledge. The brain may have memorized the table of chemical elements, may have learned to do meticulous modern surgery, may understand the stresses that could harm a bridge or large building, but may be an unmoored mind where spirit and critical thinking are concerned.

Even worse, we have found minds honed in the ancient discipline of philosophy capable of discarding humane feelings altogether. No one would consider Lenin or Pol Pot uneducated; indeed, they were well educated—yet both could engage in genocide as ruthlessly as if they were peasants slaughtering livestock.

Hitler's arsenal of executives carried out "the final solution" without a backward look at the centuries of European humanism and philosophical sophistication that made up German university education.

Radovan Karadzic, the "Butcher of Bosnia" and UN-indicted war criminal, was a practicing psychologist; the other author of genocide in Yugoslavia, Slobodan Milosevic, ex-President of Serbia and indicted war criminal, was a former banker who had spent years in New York. How did they leap from humane disciplines to murderous nationalism? This was not an aberration: Milosevic was surrounded by intellectuals espousing like-minded murderous nationalism.

We are also told that Osama bin Laden, Yasser Arafat, and most of the suicide bombers who carry out their leaders' nefarious terror policies are educated.

But perhaps we should be looking at what we mean by "educated." I remember my father commenting on my college freshman arrogance: "I can see that a little learning is a dangerous thing." That may be the key indeed. Many people who pass for educated have a lot of learning narrowly applied, while other parts of their brains are wind tunnels.

Robert Jay Lifton's depressing but fascinating book, *Destroying the World to Save It* (Lifton) is a journey through the crazy world of the irrational and often lethal new religious cults peopled by unmoored lost souls.

History of cults

Mad religious cults are nothing new in the world; our ancient ancestors who threw virgins into volcanoes to stop the eruption were certain they were right. The volcanoes did eventually stop spewing.

The Aztecs truly believed that the sun would not rise if the sun god were not fed the still-throbbing hearts of hundreds of sacrificial victims. They learned that they were wrong only after the Spaniards conquered them, and the wretched sun still came up. All that death for nothing!

The more draconian religions of the past, such as the Aztec blood sacrifice frenzy, seem to have been triggered by acts of nature that made people think their world was coming to an end. Great plagues, unusually long droughts or floods, or devastating barbarian invasions have ended the world for many people, leaving the survivors unmoored. ("Unmoored" is Lifton's term, and I find it a perfect description of a mind not anchored firmly to something dependable.)

We now know that the beginnings of the Agricultural Revolution some 10,000 years ago created societies that no longer related to the local nature gods that served the needs of hunter-gatherers. The concerns of agriculturalists now centered on sun and rain, two of the four elements of agriculture (the others being earth and human labor).

Trying to maintain agriculture in desert climates where rainfall was not dependable and the consequences of drought lethal, gave rise to gods as harsh as the environment, gods who required blood sacrifice. There is not too much difference between the concerns of the ancient Mesopotamians and the Aztecs, half a world away. Drought was real, and it killed.

The next revolution took place during what we call the Axial Age, from 600 BC to the time of Mohammad (seventh century AD). I am extending this age much longer than scholars normally do, because I think the elements of that revolution were the same.

The Axial Age began when the wealth generated by agriculture, fishing, herding, and trading became so large that a whole new class of people emerged: people who had the leisure to think. Philosophy was born during this time, not only in its Greek homeland, but also in India and China to the east, Israel to the south, and, by the end of the era, to the Roman Empire and its North African successor, the Muslim Empire.

Along with the leisure to think comes the desire to find meaning in that thinking, and it is here that religion plays a significant role. Philosophy alone does not usually drive a person to kill—or die—for that philosophy. With the exception of Socrates, I know of no philosopher who was willing to die for his thoughts. Martyrs need more red meat than philosophy, along with belief in the rewards of the hereafter.

The last epochal revolution before our own time was the Industrial Revolution, which brought with it the printing press, more materials, goods, and better and more varied foods than ever before. With it came a scientific revolution that has produced a medical revolution and a technological revolution that permits us to leave our planet for space voyages.

The communications revolution that began with the printing press is now in cyberspace, with information flashing around the globe in milliseconds. Ignorance should be on the run, one would think.

Mental compartmentalization

Alas, it is not so. Instead, we see that same mental compartmentalization again, not just in the world's handful of monsters, but in large numbers of people. It appears possible for people to master the mechanics of driving an automobile and understand why a flu shot is necessary—yet, when the Mississippi floods, they will hold hands with their pastors to pray to "God Above" to make it stop flooding. It works, doesn't it? The flood eventually recedes, just as the volcano quieted after incinerating the virgin.

It is this ability to compartmentalize, along with the "little bit of knowledge" that our educations provide to some of us, that makes possible the recruitment into the most mindless or most evil of cults.

Lifton is a psychologist with years of experience in his specialty: brainwashing and mind control, both of which were of great interest to all the players in the Cold War between the West and the former Soviet Union. The idea of a "Manchurian Candidate," someone who could be programmed to be an assassin through prolonged hypnosis, has haunted us all.

What Dr. Lifton learned was that one did not have to be hypnotized to become a monster. The Nazis used not only professional killers, but also "killing professionals," doctors such as Mengele. The World War II Japanese doctors, too, were no longer healers, but were more interested in torture and bizarre medical experiments on their war prisoners—experiments that might even have shocked ancient Assyria or Attila the Hun. [Lifton, 5]

He also learned that not every mad guru or führer is a pied piper leading children into the river, but is often a partner with his disciples. They need each other. The leader needs constant reaffirmation that he is the god he thinks he is (he is not sure), and his followers keep him alive with their adoration and obedience. Should their allegiance flag, the leader's fragile hold on sanity goes.

Lifton notes that, "I came to recognize the power of a totalized environment for mobilizing individual passions in the creation of fierce, often deeply satisfying expressions of collective energy." [Lifton, 5] People held together in a passionate environment forget they are individuals and become a body and they get a rush from their collective energy. This sounds like mob psychosis to me, except that in cults it becomes the daily norm, not just a single mindless event.

Lifton believed that the event that triggered our past half-century of murderous cults was the nuclear bombing of Hiroshima and Nagasaki. This event set off the apocalyptic fantasies that the world was coming to an end—or that these cult groups could help bring about the end.

We have an ancient religious tradition from many disparate religions about world endings, about death and resurrection, about cycles ending and new ones beginning. Perhaps the atom bomb began the latest run, but I would like to push it back to Hitler's Nazi cult.

Hitler believed that the Nazis could save the world (for themselves) by exterminating all the lesser beings, such as Jews, Gypsies, and when they could, all the dark-skinned peoples. They managed to exterminate twenty million Russians, and if their scientists had been good enough to master nuclear energy, they would have used it. When Hitler died, he would have loved to take us all with him.

Aum Shinrikyo

Lifton has charted in his book the trajectory of a Japanese cult, Aum Shinrikyo, which released sarin nerve gas on March 20, 1995, on the Tokyo subway system during morning rush hour. Had the cult's scientists been better, they could have killed hundreds of thousands instead of the eleven they killed and the 5,000 they injured.

This fanatical religious cult, presided over by a nearly blind Japanese albino named Shoko Asahara, had visions of bringing about the ancient biblical Armageddon with weapons of mass destruction. To accomplish this, they hoped to provoke their country's paranoia into believing that the destruction was coming from an outside enemy.

There are crazies right now on Afghanistan's frontier and in northern Pakistan who would love to trigger something that would get the United States and Russia to destroy each other, but they are not yet smart enough.

This Japanese group, which had left a trail of unsolved murders in its wake before getting caught after the subway attack, is part of a "loosely connected, still-developing global subculture of apocalyptic violence—or violence conceived in sweeping terms as a purification and renewal of humankind through the total or near-total destruction of the planet." [Lifton, 4]

Shoko Asahara and his cult, Aum Shinrikyo, knit together a religion that derives from a variety of sources, including a Buddhism that takes nothing from Japanese Zen, but rather from Tibetan demonism and its dark, world-destroying philosophy. Hinduism, with its concept of worlds destroyed and rebuilt in endless cycles also had great appeal for them. This seemed somehow very "New Age" to a younger generation of Japanese.

Christian apocalyptic visions also played a role in his cult, as well as in many others. Even ultra-Orthodox Jewish cults are not free of Christian apocalyptic visions today. They just hear the footsteps of a different messiah coming down the street. These cults have all plugged into an international stream of twilight zone madness.

Cult experts tell us that there are certain conditions that assist the cult in transforming individuals into a single-minded body—or rather, a body, since the guru is the mind. Adherents need absolute faith that the leader is either God or God-anointed. This assurance comes from witnessing fake miracles (Asahara was said to levitate) or from an overload of contagious enthusiasm from other adherents.

Sex is manipulated and controlled—sometimes promiscuous, sometimes renounced totally, and sometimes permitted only to the master and his chosen adherents. People such as Jim Jones (People's Temple) used sex to control chosen women. He also raped and sexually humiliated certain men in his cult to assure his control over them. [Lifton, 288]

All of these cults control food, keeping adherents borderline hungry, and control space, making privacy impossible. Sleep too is controlled, which is certainly a familiar brainwashing technique used by clandestine services the world over. These techniques are also a standard part of monastic life, both Christian and Buddhist.

The role of drugs

Drugs have played a role in initiating cult members from the time of the eleventh- and twelfth-century Persian Assassins, the first cult with murderous international reach. (The book to read is *The Assassins*, by Bernard Lewis.) The name assassin comes from hashish, or hemp, which was used on new recruits in this killer cult to get and keep them engaged. Addiction and visions are powerful motivators.

The leader of the cult, Hasan-i-Sabbah, knew that his preaching could not prevail against the entrenched orthodoxy of Sunni Islam—that his followers could not meet and defeat the armed might of the

Seljuq state. Others before him had vented their frustration in unplanned violence, in hopeless insurrection, or in sullen passivity.

Hasan found a new way, by which a small force, disciplined and devoted, could strike effectively against an overwhelmingly superior enemy. "Terrorism is carried on by a narrowly limited organization and is inspired by a sustained program of large-scale objectives in the name of which terror is practiced. This was the method that Hasan chose— the method, it may well be, that he invented." [Lewis, 130]

The role of terror

Hasan, who was called "the Old Man of the Mountain" (referring to his mountain hideout in the Alamut Castle), used a policy of assassination that kept everyone on edge. His cult claimed it could find and murder anyone, despite all precautions. [Lewis, 57].

The chief judge of Isfahan wore armor, had a bodyguard, and took precautions, but was murdered at Friday prayers in the mosque of Hamadan. Later that year (1108–09), the chief judge of Nishapur was murdered during Ramadan celebrations. In Baghdad itself, the seat of the Caliphate, the famous court minister Nizam al-Mulk was wounded but survived.

Authoritarianism

All other cults seem to have been cut from the same cloth as this mother of cults. Hasan-i-Sabbah's Shiite doctrine was authoritarian. The believer had no right of choice, but was obliged to follow the cult leader or his authorized deputy. [Lewis, 62] And, since God anointed the Imam (supposedly the descendant of the last family member of the Prophet Mohammad), men could not choose their Imam, nor could they exercise judgment in determining matters of theology and law. No democracy there.

This, of course, is the main difference between much more egalitarian Sunni Islam, in which all adult males have a voice, and Islam's minority and authoritarian Shiite sect. The effects of this difference have come down from this dark period to infect the Islamic Revolution in Iran. The Ayatollah Khomeini assumed the title of Imam and made himself the ultimate authority on theology and law, with power to trump the results of any election. It is as if a millennium of human thought and progress had not happened. The Ayatollah's authoritarianism has been taken up by the Islamist Sunnis, primarily in the organization of Al Qaeda, Osama bin Laden's group.

The role of filth

Another common element to most cults—not all, but most—is living in filth. This seems to be the ultimate defiance of orderly society. It is difficult to imagine a Japanese community living in filth when the Japanese are so clean—yet the police found the Aum facilities utterly filthy. They claimed it was their policy to kill no living creatures (a strange interpretation of extreme Buddhism). [Lifton, 32]

The Manson Family and their counterparts in the "counterculture" of the 1960s, showed their defiance of middle class hygiene and cleanliness by living in personal filth. [Lifton 274] This gave rise to a spate of venereal and other diseases that doctors working in the new free clinics had not seen in their lifetimes.

Living in filth is one way to break with the past. One way to defy Roman culture with its obsession with personal and community cleanliness was to deliberately seek its opposite. Christianity in its earliest years felt that the body needed to suffer for the soul to prevail. The early monastic movement was marked by the unbathed and lice-ridden bodies of practitioners.

The most notable distinction between Muslims and Christians in Spain and during the Crusades was the cleanliness of the former and rankness of the latter. After the Christians took back Spain from the Muslims, bathhouses were closed and one could identify a pious Christian by his or her foul odor. This is where the term "The Odor of Sanctity" comes from.

What attracts the educated to cults

It is difficult to believe that a person with education could willingly give up mental autonomy, physical cleanliness, and moral scruples, yet it seems that it happens. Critical thinking is not even on the drawing board.

What could make thirty-seven-year-old Kiyohide Hayakawa, a leader of a leftist student movement and a student of architecture and engineering, join the Aum Shinrikyo and become its "minister of construction?" [Lifton, 29] Why would a leftist develop an obsession for acquiring weapons of mass destruction from the Russians? Why would he murder? He is now in prison in Japan and has decided to turn state's evidence. Perhaps we will learn something.

Why would Ikuo Hayashi, a cardiac surgeon who had studied in the United States, leave his hospital appointment in the middle of his career and, at age forty-two (in 1988), join Aum? He became the cult's "minister of healing" and was involved in every kind of medical abuse, from extensive drugging of members and enemies to the death of some of them. [Lifton, 29]

Why would Tomomasa Nakagawa, another prominent doctor, join Aum in 1988, while still in medical school? He became the guru's personal physician, served on a murder team, and was instrumental in helping to produce the sarin nerve gas used for the Tokyo attack.

A veterinarian and graduate student in virology, Seiichi Endo joined Aum in 1989, at the age of 28. He became "minister of health and welfare," a wonderful title for someone in charge of making and using biological and chemical weapons. His skill as a scientist was as defective as his skill as a thinker, fortunately, which saved many Japanese lives from what he would have liked to do. [Lifton, 30]

Less inept was Masami Tsuchiya, a chemist with an advanced degree from Tsukuba University, a fine science school. He was the first in Aum to succeed in making sarin gas. At twenty-four he joined Aum (1989) and seems to have been deranged from the start. That he got through his science degrees is a tribute to a disassociated mind. He was wildly apocalyptic and expected Aum to take over Japan any day, according to his diaries. [Lifton, 31]

Even space science yielded one of its own to Aum. In 1989, at the age of twenty-six, Fumihiro Joyu left Japan's space agency to pursue his passion for yoga by joining Aum. He was appointed "minister of foreign affairs" and headed the large Aum operation in Russia. He was matinee-idol handsome and had a large following of women. When he leaves prison, he may become the leader of what is left of Aum. [Lifton, 31]

Japan is not the only country having trouble with mad cults. Lifton mentions the Jewish fundamentalists who encouraged the assassination of Israeli Prime Minister Yitzhak Rabin; the Palestinian Hamas suicide bombers; and Hindu and Muslim fundamentalists defending ancient "sacred" places in India. These groups will be discussed in our next chapter—Cults that Draw Upon the Ignorant. Lifton wrote before Al Qaeda burst into our lives.

American cults

Of interest to us in this chapter are Lifton's other subjects: the American apocalyptic groups such as the Charles Manson Family, Heaven's Gate, David Koresh and the Branch Davidians, People's Temple, the Oklahoma City bombers, Aryan supremacists, and paramilitary survivalists on the radical right. [Lifton, 271–302] Apocalyptic horrors have gone global like everything else, it seems.

We must assume that American cultists for the most part have some education. The Charles Manson Family was the exception, a cult of drifters with nothing in their heads but sex, drugs, and murder—all of which gave them a rush. Yet even they were taken by the idea that they could foment a great race war that would destroy America and miraculously leave them in charge.

The apocalyptic and the ridiculous are never far apart, it seems, in the brightest or most stupid among these visionaries.

The United States has a long history of religious cults and religious hysteria. This is the underbelly of the religious freedom that exists in the US, and a natural consequence of the American characteristic of re-inventing ourselves.

As a country without much of an aristocracy, and as a place where people have been on the move ever westward, there is little encrusted tradition. The half-educated pioneers who crossed the Cumberland Gap had to invent institutions that would work for them, as well as a religion that was portable and personally meaningful.

Many of these people had nothing more to read than the Bible, and had no church fathers or school of theologians to interpret these ancient texts for them. One backwater county in Kentucky recently refused to have a new library that the state was willing to provide because, as their spokesman said, "We have the Bible. We don't need any other books." He could have spoken for Davy Crockett's group in the eighteenth century as well as for his own twenty-first-century county.

The Protestant challenge to the centralized Catholic Church in the sixteenth century gave rise to ever more fragmentized Christianity, each sect interpreting the Bible its own way. This fragmentation continues today, and certainly is the reason for the rise of specialized interpretations.

There are sects in today's Bible Belt (southern and southwestern states) that focus on glossalalia—semi-trance states of hysteria in which the parishioners speak in unknown languages. Others test their faith by handling poisonous snakes under the theory that those who die in this exercise are somehow lacking in faith.

Other sects believe only in the medical treatments mentioned in the Bible: laying on of hands and anointing with oil. Their unfortunate children or other loved ones find that a burst appendix does not respond to oil, which means, of course, that this death is the will of God.

These sects are reading the Bible literally and believe that their practices are a demonstration of their utter faith. Karen Armstrong notes that the importance of religious faith is the mythic meaning, and that attempts to interpret faith literally contaminate "mythos" with "logos," wherein lies danger. [Armstrong, xiii]

Even when the Bible (or the Koran or the Zand Avesta) is interpreted literally, there is still no guarantee of uniform or consistent interpretation. There are as many interpretations as there are interpreters. The saying that the devil can quote scripture is certainly true when it comes to some of the more deadly cults. Someone clever enough can pick and choose to support even the most nefarious of actions.

Manson Family

This was both a criminal gang and an apocalyptic community. Manson preached the destruction of the bourgeois world and wanted to bring about a race war to hasten the inevitable arrival of Armageddon.

This gang of drifters invaded two mansions in Los Angeles in 1969 and butchered the inhabitants, clumsily trying to implicate Blacks. Manson, like Asahara in Japan, declared himself a god, saying, "I am the God of fuck." [Lifton, 275] Susan Atkins, one of Manson's disciples, said, "The whole world is like one big intercourse—everything is in and out—smoking, eating, stabbing." As Lifton notes, there was a communal merging of the sexual, oral, mystical, and murderous.

Manson's models for his cult were Christ and the devil (Christian theology), Hitler, Scientology, popular psychology, science fiction, and the left-hand Tantra of Hinduism, which denies the difference between good and evil. Drifter though he was, Manson was obviously quite a reader!

Manson's end of the world fantasy, however, was low-tech (murdering with knives), unlike the high-tech fantasy of the Japanese cultists.

The Bible text that seems to have done the most harm insofar as cults are concerned is the "Book of Revelations." This work is so surreal that one can find all sorts of justifications and nonsense in it. It is strange to see a work that reads like a drug-induced fantasy becoming a blueprint for cults 2,000 years later.

Jim Jones

It is easy to fool the well-meaning. A cult leader in San Francisco whose stated purpose was racial harmony and concern for the poor received much adulation from city officials and the radial chic in San Francisco society. During his beginnings in Indiana, Jones attracted mostly what one would expect of a Pentecostal community: working class Whites. When he moved to the West Coast, the group started to attract well-educated White students and professionals, as well as urban middle-class Blacks.

Jim Jones and his People's Temple were featured in numerous media publications and television documentaries. He was too good to be true. What his admirers did not know was that this once Pentecostal preacher had begun to mistake himself for God. When it appeared that the press might start to look harder, he moved his cult to Guyana, a backwater country on the northeast coast of South America.

Terrible stories began to seep out of Guyana to cult members' families in California. When California Congressman Ryan went to Guyana to have a look, he and several of his aides were murdered at Jones' panicky command.

His utopian fantasy was soon blown wide open for the world to see. Suicide and murder took a toll of 913 in Jonestown, four in Georgetown nearby, and, of course, the five in Congressman Ryan's party.

The murders and suicide were low-tech: grape-flavored Kool-Aid® (laced with potassium cyanide), guns, and knives. The cyanide, of course, was a nice Nazi touch, quite appropriate for a cult with a leader who saw himself as God.

Lifton compares Jones with Asahara, and there are indeed similarities, as there are with Charles Manson. All were poor and had marginalized childhoods; all had talent as religious demagogues, leaders, and con men; and all were psychologically volatile, pendulum swinging from enormously loving to icily cruel. They were all Christ and anti-Christ, God and anti-God. That is how they saw themselves and how their followers saw them.

All of these movements seem to have been influenced by the horror of—and fascination with—a nuclear war bringing the world to an end. They all had powerful feelings of hatred toward society and their own countries, combined with a passion for (and obviously ignorance of) socialism.

All three of these cult leaders used control of human needs to dominate their disciples. Hunger, sleep-deprivation, dirty living conditions, and, above all, sexual abuse kept everyone in line. Sex could be used to elevate or demean followers. Most peculiar was the idea of sexual license for the gurus but (except for the Manson family) sexual deprivation for everyone else.

Whether death by world destruction or by suicide, death is the end of such cults. The leader's psyche implodes, and everything goes. One is reminded of Hitler's end—an end he would much rather have shared with the world if he could.

As the end of our self-proclaimed millennium approached in the late 1990s, all sorts of suicide, genocide, and omnicide fantasies emerged from the fringes of the world's societies.

Branch Davidians

We have seen supposedly educated people involved in these disasters. The David Koresh cult in Waco, Texas, led by a man as wildly deranged as the three described above, courted a shootout with authorities, which ended suicidally in a fiery holocaust. Koresh was obsessed with the Bible's "Book of Revelations," as are so many others of his ilk.

Koresh, like the other gurus discussed above, progressed from preacher to inflated god-priest who demanded absolute obedience from his followers. He too used sex to control members, as well as millennial fantasies and end-of-the-world, self-fulfilling scenarios. Those members who defected or tried to avoid the suicidal end were dispatched by bullet.

Miscellaneous crazies

In 1999 the Israeli government was on the lookout for mad cultists who would descend upon Jerusalem intending to bring about the end of the world. These cultists hoped to start a full-scale war between Arabs and Israelis that would then drag in the rest of the world. The cultists did not succeed in provoking a major conflagration, but ultra-nationalist Israelis and Palestinians needed no help from the outside to continue killing each other.

Heaven's Gate

Thirty-nine cultists from a group known as Heaven's Gate committed mass suicide in 1997. This seemingly gentle group that supported itself with computer technical service did not plan to destroy the world, but rather to leave it by hitching a ride on a wandering space ship that they expected to swing by on the tail of a comet. How could the seemingly educated members of this cult have believed such a thing?

Although this cult did not seem as violent as many of their fellow cults, there was enough violence to go around. Cult members were encouraged to castrate themselves (a good old early Christian practice), a practice that was not easy to do since most medical doctors would refuse to do this. The cult was not around long enough to recruit doctors who might put their scruples aside.

There are many other UFO cults around that have not yet made the news with fatally bizarre behavior. At least they are not yet "doing it in the street and frightening the horses," as our Edwardian ancestors would have said.

Guns and Bible

The more remote areas of the American west are home to small cults of "survivalists," such as the notorious Weaver family living on Ruby Ridge, Montana, who engaged in a shootout with federal agents.

These cultists believe that the end of the world is coming, and that if they play it right, they may be the survivors. Armed with the "Book of Revelations," a hatred for the secular government of the United States (and all officials therein), stockpiles of food, and most of all, an enormous arsenal of guns, these people are prepared to hold off the forces that they think will descend on them after a nuclear holocaust. They are, in effect, the newest kind of warlords.

These groups share a belief in a very masculine Christianity that dislikes the pacifism of Jesus Christ and they consider any government that calls for religious, racial, and gender equality a rebellion against God and Jesus. "Our God is not a wimp. He's the God of righteousness and wrath." [Lifton, 328]

Timothy McVeigh, the perpetrator of the bombing of the federal building in Oklahoma City in 1995, served enthusiastically in the Persian Gulf War where he happily boasted of killing Iraqis running from their trenches, and then began to demonstrate his rabid racism and obsession with nuclear disaster and Communist attacks, which put an end to his military career.

Along with his selective reading of the Bible, McVeigh was sucked in by another book that had become the new bible of the survivalist, paramilitary, neo-Nazi, and White racist millenarians: *The Turner Diaries*. This is an apocalyptic neo-Nazi novel that dramatizes a White revolution in America that leads to a global nuclear holocaust in which, conveniently, only Jews and non-Whites are exterminated.

The author of this vicious book, William Pierce, who assumed the pseudonym of Andrew MacDonald, is a former professor at Oregon State University with a doctorate in physics. He headed a Nazi youth club and wrote this dreadful work in serial form to be published in the group's journal, *Attack!*

One may well wonder what he studied on his path toward his doctorate! From where in his mind did the idea come that conceives of a "hero" who drops a small nuclear bomb on the Pentagon to save the White American revolution? [Lifton, 332] The murderous combination of racism and pseudo-spirituality (akin to Hitler's Aryan "spirituality" with the whiff of Valkyries whisking the heroes' bodies to some White paradise) is a great stretch from the critical thinking and humanistic tradition that one would think of as intellectual.

Fortunately for us, relatively few people are involved in such cults. Unfortunately, it does not take many people to produce enormous pain and devastation. We will continue to see such cults as a poisonous undercurrent in a world that otherwise is on the threshold of enormous mental, medical, astronomical, and social leaps forward that promise enormous fulfillment for humankind.

There's a sucker born every minute.
                                    —David Hannum

Chapter 5.
Cults enlisting the ignorant

iteracy and ignorance are not mutually exclusive, as can be seen
from the materials presented in Chapter 4. People may know how
to read without knowing how to think, how to interpret what they read,
or how to protect themselves from con men.

Indeed, some of the most unfortunate victims of religious cult leaders
read only the Bible, or the Koran, or the Book of Mormon, and, while
they may be able to quote chapter and verse, they do not really understand what they have read.

My favorite story to illustrate this is the cult in Kenya that believed
that their Christian faith could be demonstrated by emulating Jesus and
walking on water. Those who performed this exercise, of course,
drowned. However, this did not deter the other cult members from
remaining hopeful.

The United States, with its long history of religious freedom and
religious eccentricity, has more than its fair share of ignorant cults. Faith
healers and snake-oil salesmen are a sizeable part of our religious history.
There has always been money to be made from the gullibility—and
vulnerability— of the ignorant.

In the nineteenth century, faith healing was an expected part of
revival evangelism. Rough-hewn sinners living on the ever-moving fron-
tiers paused from their drinking, gambling, and whoring and returned
for a moment to their imagined childhoods. Public confession of sin,
being washed in the blood of the lamb, and dropping money in the
passed hat gave them a hope of salvation. These people were saved, and
saved again, and saved yet again. Hope springs eternal.

We have indeed had our Elmer Gantrys, our Amy Semple
McPhersons, and—our newest variety—the televangelists who bilk

money out of lonely widows with extraordinary religious gullibility. In the late 1990s, con artists in twenty-seven states had taken advantage of at least ninety thousand investors who believe that faith in God is synonymous with faith in the investment scam. Deceived investors lost more than $1.8 billion. One such religious con man in Florida was sentenced to twenty-seven years in prison; five officials from the Baptist Foundation of Arizona were indicted on thirty-two counts of theft, fraud, and racketeering. [*SFC*, 8/8/01]

There are religious cults in our neighborhoods that never attract attention until disaster strikes. There are abusers of children who are just following the Bible, they say. There are wife beaters who can refer to all the religious texts in the world to justify their right. There are assassins and self-appointed executioners whose targets are women who refuse to cover up, remain silent, or submit. Not that any of this is new, but that it should be so active an industry in our supposedly enlightened time is disheartening.

The range of ignorance runs the gamut from people who can read but do not think to people who are truly ignorant in every way. We will start with the former group, most of whom are in the United States, and will then travel throughout the world to some very unexpected places.

Cults in America
Christianity à la carte
One reads frequently about people who belong to cults with strange interpretations of Christianity or what they think is Christianity.

In 1977, cult member Mason McKinley from Oakland, California, was told by his minister that he should give up his baby daughter and let his wife divorce him. [*SFC*, 9/12/00] After years of devotion, he was compelled to leave the cult. The "church" is "The Spiritual Rights Foundation" and the "Academy for Psychic Studies" is its seminary (in Berkeley). Members give a third of their earnings to their leader, Bill Duby, forcing some into bankruptcy. The church, however, owns considerable real estate, in addition to many Cadillacs and businesses.

Former members now say that children are hypnotized, schooling is an afterthought, and fathers are purposely alienated from their children. There is, as with most cults, a cloud of highly charged sexual tension.

McKinley came from a moral family that taught him to do as he was told. He was a Boy Scout, graduated from a university, and then fell right into this cult—he was interested in spiritual and paranormal things.

The minister's background was lower class and unhappy. He was a drifter, and soon found a guru: Michael Ehrlich, a convicted swindler known as Marc Reymont who was a late night television psychic. (Ehrlich was bludgeoned to death in Oakland in 1982.)

Duby founded the "Spiritual Rights Foundation," based on the "philosophy" that we are surrounded by "foreign energy" and "family programming" from earthbound entities. Hugging is discouraged because it transfers energy, and sex is closely monitored by "Reverent Bill."

What is most distressing is that McKinley didn't even realize he had spent fourteen years in a cult until he picked up a book in a bookstore while waiting for his laundry next door. He is now suing for total custody of his daughter.

Other cults around the country read the Bible selectively to defend beating children with supposed demonic possession (not infrequently to the point of death). Some reject modern medicine and opt for laying on of hands, prayer, and anointing with oil. Members of such cults live otherwise contemporary lives. The death rate for their children (and the number of children born to couples who do not practice modern medicine) is well above the national norm.

The following is representative of this problem: a nationwide manhunt ended October 5, 1998, after searchers found a malnourished child at a remote campsite in Montana. [SFC, 10/6/98] His parents, claiming he was the Christ Child, were hiding him after kidnapping him from a Utah hospital, an FBI spokesman said. The baby previously had been taken by health officials from his deranged parents and hospitalized for severe malnutrition; he was twenty months old, but weighed what a six-month-old would weigh.

Relatives of the baby said that he had been fed a diet of lettuce and watermelon to keep his body "pure" because his parents believed he was either the Christ Child or a prophet.

In another similar case, [SFC, 22/14/00] the leader of a fundamentalist sect and his wife were indicted on murder charges in November, 2000, in the death of their infant son who, authorities believe, died of starvation. A third member of the sect was charged as an accessory. This sect does not believe in modern medicine or in our legal system. A father turned state's evidence and blew the whistle, leading authorities to the graves of this baby as well as his own child. The sect leaders believed that a "vision" told them to starve the baby. They would walk by his crib and watch his eyes roll in his head and see his ribs, and then go eat dinner.

Faulty Bible interpretation has led to other strange cases. From Alabama, we find the following: "If the Rev. James Henderson has his way, the division of church and state in this tiny hamlet (Brooksville, Alabama) will be so narrow, a single Bible verse, 'Love thy neighbor,' would cover it."

A group of Henderson's cult members wants to form a town, "but not one in which mortal elected officials would have the power to hand out liquor licenses, levy taxes and rezone land for strip malls and industrial parks." They want a town governed by the hand of God.

The King James Bible would be the town charter, the Ten Commandments its ordinances. Voting—infrequent voting—would be done in church. [*SFC*, 1/2/99]

From even closer to my neighborhood came this strange story: a father was arrested because he chained his three sons to their bedposts to keep them from killing him as he slept. John Davis (the father) says God and the Bible instructed him to be strict with his children so they wouldn't grow up to kill him and his wife.

"Proverbs tells you to discipline your children, or else they will grow up and kill their parents," Davis said. "All I did was discipline them."

He obviously tortured his children, and the children responded by trying to commit suicide. One of the three died after eating some drywall (and before he could be taken to a doctor, Davis said.)

The other two boys blew the whistle on their parents and had them arrested. The children were malnourished, underdeveloped, and scarred from whippings, and also had marks on their wrists from restraints. It does not seem that literacy did the father much good. [*SCS*, 10/24/00]

Even the US Congress can be fooled by the supposed good works of a religious person. The 1999 "Parent of the Year Award," an honor created by Congress in 1994, was bestowed on a Colorado man with connections to a cult that once prostituted its female members as "happy hookers for Jesus."

Moreover, the National Parents Day Foundation, which chooses the annual winner, has been found to have ties to the Rev. Sun Myung Moon and his Unification Church. So much for "faith-based" charities.

The recipient, Zack Prendergast of Longmont, Colorado, returned the award when questions were raised about his involvement with the Children of God (locally known as "happy hookers"), a group that was started in California by David Berg in the 1960s. The group eventually went worldwide after Berg fled tax evasion charges and led his followers out of the country. They became infamous when, in addition to prostituting female members, they were linked to child pornography in South America.

Taking on a new name, "The Family," a number of its adherents have returned to the US, where they will undoubtedly find many new recruits. [*SCS*, 8/5/99]

In my own neighborhood, there are people who claim that an angel appeared to them and left its image on a chunk of oak in their garden. [*SCS*, 7/18/99]

We not only have our own local folly, but we ship it abroad too. In January of 1999, Israeli police detained eight adults and six children belonging to an apocalyptic Christian sect from Denver and said the group intended to carry out violent acts in Jerusalem to hasten the second coming of Christ.

This group abandoned their homes and jobs in Colorado and headed to Jerusalem to await the millennium. The group called itself "Concerned Christians" and their charismatic leader had the good sense to stay in Colorado, letting his followers face what he hoped would be the Apocalypse.

The leader, Monte Kim Miller, a forty-four-year-old former marketing executive for Procter & Gamble, predicted that Denver would be destroyed in a powerful earthquake in October (it was not), and also prophesied that he would die violently on the streets of Jerusalem in the final days of 1999 (he did not.) However, false or stupid prophecy did not deter his gullible followers. They were expelled from Israel and are now back in Denver. [*SFC*, 1/4/99]

Voodoo

Christianity is not the only home for American religious folly. It would not be surprising to hear of African Voodoo practices in Haiti or Brazil, but I was surprised recently to hear on National Public Radio of the growth of the Santorian cult (a pseudo-African religion) in Florida, where an obviously educated and well-spoken Santorian "priest" was blessing a follower's new car by sacrificing a chicken and anointing the car hood with its blood.

Black Muslims

The Black Muslim movement has spawned many sub-cults as well, with their own interpretations of Islamic law. One fanatical adherent, Kenneth Earl Tyson, was arrested in San Francisco for killing his girl-friend in a fit of rage after she would not wear Muslim-style attire when she served as maid of honor at her best friend's wedding.

His girlfriend was staying with her mother for the wedding party (she lives in Sacramento). Tyson, also known as Kenneth Sharif, had been the girl's boyfriend since they met in 1997, while she was still in high school. "Tyson was a stickler for adherence to the Muslim faith, insisting on the proper way to dress and pray," said an acquaintance. [*SFC*, 12/15/00]

Mormons

Renegade Mormon fundamentalists in Colorado City, Arizona, are pulling their children out of public schools and have cut off communications with outsiders and former church members.

The Mormon Church has been looking the other way as fringe polygamy continues in Utah and Arizona. Word has it that one big issue is the Second Coming of Christ. These fundamentalists are very apocalyptic. But another issue is their fierce belief that polygamy is a "principle" that they are willing to defend to their death. [*SFC*, 9/17/00]

They fail to note that polygamy was a Mormon practice during the time that the cult was in its formative years and women outnumbered men. It is today illegal, yet these renegades think they have a direct pipeline to God.

Voluntary religious practices should not be subjected to societal interference in our tolerant society, except when children are coerced, beaten, and given in marriage without their consent. This issue has already reached the courts in Utah and achieved notoriety throughout the United States when youngsters fled to the police and blew the whistle on these peculiar cults.

Amish and Mennonites

The Amish and Mennonites, cults with roots in the seventeenth century, have lived in isolation from the rest of society. They have established communities that conform to their own vision of Christianity in the United States, Canada, and Mexico. They have for the most part flourished on a regime of careful agriculture, avoidance of electricity and automobiles except for agricultural use, and strict control over family life. Modern medicine and modern entertainments have been rejected, and yet, because of the basically healthy lifestyle of good food, good work, and wholesome pleasures, they have certainly survived despite their isolation.

Recently, however, there have been signs of these cults coming apart at last. Young people are showing signs of rebellion to the point that drug addiction and drug trafficking have become a major problem. It appears that the communications revolution cannot be kept at bay forever. The cults in Mexico are having a particularly bad time with drug trafficking among the young and the police are intervening. [*SCS*, 1/28/01]

Ultra-Orthodox Jews

Some ultra-Orthodox Jewish cults, like the Amish and Mennonites and fundamentalist Mormons, depend upon isolation to keep their vision of religion pristine. Communities have sprung up in rural New York and as far afield as Iowa and Palo Alto, California. The children are strictly controlled, as are the women, and the only study worthy of pursuit is reading the Torah. This leaves the students (most of them male) quite unprepared for the real world.

Of late, some of these communities—both in the United States and in Israel—have been looking ever more cult-like. Leaders enjoy a reverence (and income) that should make the thoughtful wary. In New York, members of a powerful Jewish cult that was presided over by a Rabbi Menachem Mendel Schneerson had worked themselves into a frenzy with the notion that their rabbi was the long-awaited Messiah. He died in 1994, and the miracles that should have followed his demise did not occur. The sect, however, continues. [Armstrong, 213]

There have been several cases of cult rabbis engaging in large-scale fraud. A rabbi in San Francisco, who presided over a community of ultra-Orthodox Russian-Jewish immigrants, was prosecuted for his criminal financial activities, and yet the very people who had been fleeced begged for leniency from the court. They said it would be a hardship for their community to continue without him.

Four other rabbis who bilked the US government out of $40 million in education aid, housing subsidies, and small-business loans, all in support of a non-existent religious school, were inexplicably given a presidential pardon by President Clinton in January, 2001. [*Time*, 2/5/01, p 28.] Apparently their piety does not extend to theft from the government or their own gullible followers.

Elsewhere Around the World
Israel
Israel is home to some of the best-educated and smartest people in the world, as is the United States. However, both countries have problems with undereducated people who are in thrall to their notion of religion, and they have erupted out of the twilight zone.

One particularly troublesome political party in the Israeli parliament is the ultra-Orthodox "Shas." This is not only a political party, but is a social movement representing a distinct counterculture, and, according to Suzanne Zima, [*SFC*, 7/13/00] its goal is to turn back the clock.

"The Shas is now the unrivaled vanguard of the uneducated, mainly religious Sephardim (Jews from the Arab world), who sit on one side of Israel's great divide—hardly within shouting distance of the Ashkenazim, the educated, Westernized, mainly secular Jews of European origin," said Zima.

The head of the Tami Steinmetz Center for Peace Research at Tel Aviv University notes that the question of state versus religion has not been resolved since the early days of Israel.

The Shas, by any account, is undemocratic, anti-Western and antagonistic to modern state institutions. Its ethos, values, and culture are antithetical to the rule of law and authority of the state.

Its leader exercises virtually dictatorial authority over the Shas membership and he does not like Israel's high court. He wants the

Torah to be the law of the land, and urges his followers to come to rabbis for disputes. (Note the parallel with the Alabama town that wants the Bible to be the town charter.)

This party is not fighting for equal opportunity, equal education, or redress of societal wrongs. They are fighting for a separate culture to keep their old ways. A senior fellow at the Israel Democracy Institute calls the Shas "the politics of resentment," which bears a striking resemblance to Iran's Shiites.

The members rely on amulets carrying special blessings—and curses are heaped on foes. The people believe in these magical amulets and curses, and pay good money to the rascals who provide them. (I recall the comment of a US Air Force pilot who, while flying over Texas heard a radio advertisement for "an autographed picture of Jesus Christ for only $10!")

The former Shas leader is under indictment for taking bribes of $155,000 as well as fraud, breach of trust, and moral turpitude, yet his followers are agitating for his release and are waiting to be fleeced again.

Even stranger is the latest fascination of the ultra-Orthodox with reincarnation, a concept not found in Judaism. [*SFC*, 8/6/00] On August 6, 2000, in Jerusalem, a rabbi who heads the biggest ultra-Orthodox political party said the six million Jews who perished in the Nazi Holocaust died because they were reincarnations of sinners. He also declared that the Palestinians are "snakes." He called the Nazis evil and the victims poor people, but said they were the souls of sinners, people who transgressed and did all sorts of things that should not be done. They had been reincarnated to atone. Educated Israelis are furious.

This neo-mystical fixation of the ultra-Orthodox has fueled an enormous market in "trinkets and tombs," reminiscent of medieval church rackets in "relics and pilgrimages." [*CSM*, 6/29/99]

Some Israelis are going for mystical cults and reverence for rabbinical "saints." One such saint, Baba Sali, a rabbi who died in 1984, has a shrine where people go to ask for intervention with God. (Chaucer's Canterbury Tales comes to mind.) A new big business has been built on the "intervention" of tsadiks (dead holy men), the blessings of living holy men, and sales of protective amulets.

There has been a revival of interest in the medieval mystical cult of the Kabbalah in Israel, without the sophistication of the old Kabbalah cult. In today's incarnation, superstition is the main element and the Shas party is using it to bring in money. During the late 1990s the Shas' parliamentary representation went from ten to seventeen seats.

Shas campaigned by handing out amulets and voting instructions. Exorcisms were creating problems too. An unusually rational Shas Party government minister explained: "There is only one way to bring people to Judaism, and that is through the Torah, not magic. There are many charlatans who exploit people, and we give legitimacy to this when we deliver amulets to people." Are Israelis starved for spiritual nourishment?

The biblical Sabbatical, "not to sow thy field, nor prune thy vineyard," has caused a big fight in Israel, led by an ultra-Orthodox rabbi suffering more from literalism than ignorance. [*CSM*, 9/12/00] Israeli farmers have gotten around the Sabbatical by selling their land on paper to non-Jews for the year, with the blessings of the Chief Rabbi. Now the ultra-Orthodox rabbi of Jerusalem has threatened to excommunicate the Chief Rabbi, who is afraid—has been confronted by death threats and a newspaper editorial that did not even grant him the honorific of Rabbi! Politicians have stepped in to allow each community to do what it sees as best, but secularists are now fully aware that this is war.

Burma

One of the strangest cults to emerge out of the already dreadful military dictatorship of Burma (Myanmar) revolves around the story of a pair of adolescent twin boys born into the persecuted Karen tribe, a very superstitious fringe Christian group in rebellion against Burma. [*SFC*, 1/19/01]

The Karen National Union rebels have been locked in a life-and-death struggle for survival against Burma for decades. Three years ago, two stunted twin boys, Johnny and Luther Htoo, became their leaders. Their followers thought that the children were invulnerable to bullets on the battlefield, a belief supported by sheer luck in a few anti-government raids.

The international press got wind of this story when a photographer showed these undersized, chain-smoking urchins toting M-16 rifles almost as big as they are. Their organization called itself "God's Army."

It is unclear how this fundamentalist Christian group took hold in a predominantly Buddhist country.

Despite the fervor of their mystical belief, hunger ultimately drove the children and a handful of followers into Thailand, where they surrendered. The children were reunited with their mother in a Karen refugee camp.

Rastafarians

Rastafarians belong to a sect that has surfaced among Blacks in the Caribbean Islands. Some have attained fame as singers and entertainers, which, along with their long curly "dreadlocks," has attracted attention in the United States. The sect long seemed benign.

Lately, however, they have made news with some extremely bizarre behavior. Two Rastafarian cult members attacked a Catholic cathedral on St. Lucia, a small Caribbean island, setting it ablaze with more than 400 people inside and killing a nun. They told police they were sent by God to combat corruption in the Roman Catholic Church. They were denounced by Rastafarian authorities. [*SCS*, 1/2/01]

While this may have just been the action of individuals who were deranged, another Rastafarian movement is afoot that speaks of organized folly. [*CSM*, 12/21/00] African Americans of the Rastafarian faith are heading to Ethiopia because they have the notion that they are returning to their "African Roots." This notion is, of course, without substance. The majority of Africans brought to the New World were from West Africa, not from Ethiopia.

When they arrive in their promised land (Ethiopia), they find poverty, unemployment, and general misery. Undeterred, however, they regard the late Emperor Haile Selassi as the new Messiah. One of their beliefs is that marijuana is a sacred herb and that God commanded them to use it as a means for achieving closeness to God.

This is an astonishing hodgepodge of nonsense, and is having unfortunate consequences for the innocents who sold their earthly possessions to move back to "the homeland."

The Philippines

The Philippines have enough of a gulf between the educated and the ignorant without their latest problem, a new, and very ignorant Muslim rebel sect in the southern Philippines. [*SFC*, 5/9/00] According to

David Lamb, "In its short, violent history, the Abu Sayyaf rebel group has left a trail of death and kidnappings in the southern Philippines, but has done little to advance its announced goal of creating a 'pure' Islamic state.

"Its tactics include extortion, assassination and kidnapping for ransom. Hundreds of people have died as a result, villages have been razed, and civilians have been terrorized. Although Abu Sayyaf is believed to have no more than 200 armed followers, they have managed to evade army units that are ten times larger in the jungles of Jolo Island."

Abu Sayyaf is a new group, led by someone who had been "educated" by the Saudis and given military training in Libya and Afghanistan. He is obviously deranged. He wants to create a breakaway state ruled only by the Koran, or at least his notion of the Koran.

Traditional Filipino Muslims are shocked and non-Muslims are very angry. The struggle has apparently reached Manila in a series of car and bus bombings that are reminiscent of the Palestinian Intifada and the Lebanese civil war of the 1980s. It is all inexplicable and outrageous and is not bringing new recruits to Islam.

A naive American convert to Islam (from Oakland, California) thought that he could "dialogue" with the Abu Sayyef group. He walked into their camp where they promptly imprisoned him and it appears that he will not survive the ordeal. Dialogue with religious fanaticism is a thankless task.

Uganda

The number of cults with a suicidal end is growing. In the past, there have been cults that urged celibacy to the point of cult extinction over time. The Shakers were such a cult. However, the new cults opting for extinction in our own time are much more violent in their execution, including murder of those cult members unwilling to commit suicide. The Jim Jones cult in Jonestown was one of these. Now Uganda is another.

In March, 2000, reports began to come out of Uganda that a number of people in a cult died in a church that was doused in gasoline. [*SFC*, 3/20/00]

This cult was founded in 1989 by former Catholic priests and nuns. The Virgin Mary had supposedly appeared before this former priest (Joseph Kibwetere) in a vision. He was to found a mission devoted to living by the Ten Commandments. He also claimed the world would end Dec. 31, 1999, and when it did not, he pushed it back a year to 2000. The cultists did not even wait until New Year's Eve, however.

As more information filtered out, it seems the sect was actually started by a former prostitute. The estimate of the number of dead was increased from 300 to 470. [AP, 3/20/00] By March 24, investigators found that most of the deaths were caused by foul play, not suicide. [*SFC*, 3/24/00]

Authorities now believe that the fire was set by the cult's religious leaders, unbeknownst to the members who died. Six people were murdered the day before and thrown into toilet pits.

Conjecture is that the leadership may have decided to stave off a revolt of disenchanted followers by killing all of them. There is increasing speculation that the top leader, 68-year-old Joseph Kibwetere, may be alive and that he managed to flee the country after masterminding the killings. The murdered six were poisoned, beaten, and their faces doused with acid, making identification impossible.

Relatives have said many cult members were ready to leave and wanted their money back. Both the bank account and the prophecy were bankrupt.

China

One interesting cult that deserves closer scrutiny is the Falun Gong, a movement whose leader lives in safety in the United States while his followers are arrested and beaten by the Chinese police.

Defenders of "religious freedom" around the world have found a wonderful cause in showing a peaceful, gentle religious movement being persecuted by the atheist Chinese Communist government. The Chinese government, which may have right on its side, looks like a bully as flashbulbs pop when passive resisters are beaten by the police.

The movement is described as an eclectic blend of meditation, martial arts, and visualization techniques, which sounds benign enough, but with an adored cult leader living in safety outside of China, there is cause for concern. The "visualization techniques" may be a form of mind control, in which people are mentally prepared to die for their "cause." [*SFC*, 5/10/99]

According to Orville Schell, a respected UC Berkeley China expert, the Chinese government may indeed have reason for concern. This cult is feared because there are so many stories in Chinese history about these kinds of millenarian-like movements being harbingers of dynastic collapse. It has great symbolic meaning. There is a notion that the mandate of heaven confers the right to rule until certain phenomena point to failing cosmic sanction. That could be an earthquake, a peasant rebellion, or the rise of a folk cult claiming special spiritual powers.

On the practical level, however, it is alarming to have a sizeable number of people hooked by a cult that has the capability of controlling their actions and detaching them from reason and autonomy. That is obviously a danger with cults—and particularly with the Falun Gong cult.

Freedom to read

To conclude this sad chapter, there is another issue that one would hope could serve as a countermeasure to cult recruitment, and that is reading and critical thinking.

The Catholic Index of Forbidden Texts emerged with the printing press. The Church was concerned about the rising tide of literacy among people they felt were too innocent to think, and the Index was their response to this problem. This was an effective tactic for the Catholic world until well after World War II, when it lost its effectiveness.

The mind-controllers today come from other religions. Egypt, which was once the beacon of comparative freedom from religious pressure in the Muslim world has now knuckled under in the face of growing Islamist violence.

Every year, millions of people attend the Cairo International Book Fair where they have access to everything from Western classics to Arabic poetry and school texts. [*CSM*, 1/29/01]

At the fair, there are symposia on politics, religion, and economy, an unusual opportunity for democratic dialogue in a region that is increasingly inhospitable to such freedom.

This year, the Ministry of Culture stopped printing three contemporary Egyptian novels, calling them "obscene." Secular writers are worried because they see this as one more loss of freedom to religious fanatics. They are correct. Several weeks before the fair, an Egyptian writer, Salaheddin Mohsen was sentenced to three years in jail with hard labor for "blasphemy against Islam."

In Iran, where the battle for freedom of thought is reaching revolutionary pitch, thirty pro-reform magazines have been closed down and their journalists jailed. "It will be great danger to the national security and people's faith if the enemies of the Islamic Revolution control or infiltrate the press," said Ayatollah Khomeini. [*SFC*, 8/600]

Morocco banned three independent newspapers in December after they published a letter implicating the prime minister in a 1972 coup attempt against the former king.

"There are freedoms," said Egyptian President Hosni Mubarak, "but they can't contradict our traditions. We must guarantee that freedom of expression agrees with our values."

This statement reminds one of a remark made by another Islamist: that women should have full freedom, just so long as it is within four walls.

Fortunately for freedom of thought, the three banned novels can be read on the Internet. Like the revolutionary changes that followed the advent of the printing press, revolutionary changes will rise out of the Internet.

One final and more cheerful note: in Israel, the ultra-Orthodox have waged an ugly campaign to keep Jewish women from reading the Torah at the Wailing Wall. The men hurl epithets and furniture at the women, and the women have taken it to the Israeli high court. In a groundbreaking decision, the Supreme Court ruled in May of 2000 that women may read aloud from the Torah at the Western Wall, Judaism's holiest site.

The ultra-Orthodox hated it and wanted to overrule the court. Anat Hoffman, with the organization "Women of the Wall," called the ruling a turning point in a society where the ultra-Orthodox control even civil functions such as death and marriage ceremonies. "I was ashamed that I lived in a city and belonged to a religion where a woman who prays there could be imprisoned for half a year." The court has alerted the civil authorities to make arrangements to protect the women.

This is a candle to light the darkness. Once more, religious ideology is spawning war. The book to read on this topic is *On the Causes of War,* by Michael Andregg, Ground Zero Minnesota, Minneapolis, 1999.

"Jihad universities" in Yemen

Yemen, which may rival north Pakistan and the Taliban's Afghanistan in the misery and ignorance of its population, is host to five institutions that are serving as the ideological wings of a Middle East terror network controlled by Osama bin Laden. These Dar al-Hadith schools (meaning gateway to the Sayings of the Prophet Mohammad) are run by Sheik Muqbel bin Hadi al-Wadie, who was naive enough to permit some journalists to visit. [*CSM*, 2/6/01]

The schools are spartan indeed, with dormitories nothing more than hovels made of mud bricks, and food equally spartan. In the case of the miserable madrasas in Pakistan, the young boys in the student body find more food there than they would receive at home and at least have a modicum of care. Not so in Yemen.

But the astonishing case with the schools in Yemen is that they are attracting foreigners—Americans, Europeans, Egyptians, Somalis, and Libyans. One young Englishman was interviewed by the reporters. "We do everything in conformity with the Koran here, and if you don't do the same you will burn in a hell sixty-nine times hotter than this desert," he said.

The "students" walk to their classes with Kalashnikovs on their backs and hooked daggers in their belts. What they learn can be gathered from the above interview. It does not look like universal learning to me.

Students and teachers from Yemen, Somalia, Britain, and the US talked about their concept of Jihad (holy war). They all insist that they only advocate "right" Jihad—and that excludes all forms of terrorism. They deny, of course, having had anything to do with the terrorist bombing of the USS Cole in Yemen's Aden Harbor in October 2000.

The school has its own strict interpretation of the Koran and believes its mission is to spread Islam across the world.

The Yemeni government is afraid to crack down on these schools because everyone is armed and ready to fight. Many of the militants in these schools returned from Afghanistan and then fought for the Yemeni government in its war against the Marxist southern secessionists in 1994, a war that they won, much to Yemen's misfortune. There are also new recruits from Chechnya's fight with Russia.

One might wonder how much of the recruitment is fueled by the same testosterone, thuggery, boredom and, perhaps, desperation, that once peopled the French Foreign Legion.

To paraphrase Mae West, who once announced that "goodness has nothing to do with it, dearie," in these schools, apparently, "education has nothing to do with it."

In all ages of the world, priests have been enemies of liberty.
　　　　　—David Hume, 1711–76
　　　　　　　　　Essays, Moral, Political, and Literary,
　　　　　　　　　"Of the Parties of Great Britain," (1741–2)

Chapter 6.
Twisted thinking

An idea much repeated in our time is that literacy is the cure for all that ails the world. The United Nations considers the spread of literacy an indispensable element of social development. It is certainly clear that countries with high literacy do better materially than those with low literacy, and it is also clear that countries with less than 50 percent literacy cannot sustain democracy. [The book to see is *Prospects of Democracy: A study of 172 countries,* by Tatu Vanhanen, Routledge, 1997.]

As an intellectual and lifelong book lover myself, it has been a matter of faith to me that being able to read is key to being able to think. I never considered, however, how twisted thinking could become. Literacy is neither enough to protect us from evil nor are all ideas good ideas.

There is so much that we owe to intellect: the scientific process in which theories are tested and the results documented; the harnessing of energy to do the human tasks that once enslaved men, women (property), and draft animals; the system of governance that involves input from all adults; the variety of religious faiths from which we may all choose or may avoid without punishment; the abundance of modern foods and medicines that make us the healthiest human beings who ever lived on this planet; and, of course, the freeing of humans from gravity with the advent of space travel.

Bit by bit, since the advent of the printing press and the industrial revolution, the educated elite in the world has propelled all the above changes in governance, religion, technology, and mindset. The fruit of these changes has been a global system in which there is instant communication, a global economy that provides for our plenty, and a growing concept of democratic governance based on secular thought.

Literacy is indeed wonderful, but it is not always a safeguard against dreadful twisted thinking. Intellectuals may have learned to think, but this thinking does not necessarily lead to good ends. Brilliance is not a guaranteed defense against evil thoughts.

Intellectual evil

A backward glance at the twentieth century can show us how much evil has come out of people who were well trained in thinking and reason. Many of the followers of Hitler were educated in what was thought to be one of the finest intellectual systems in the world: the German universities.

Who could have guessed that a doctor trained in humane German medicine could conceive of using his training to conduct savage "experiments" on concentration camp children? Dr. Mengele seems to have had little difficulty in using his healing skills for torture, nor did he use the critical thinking in which he was schooled—presumably in German humanism—in following a system as vicious as Naziism.

The same can be said for the Japanese doctors and their obscene medical tortures during World War II. Those doctors were either trained in Europe or in Japanese universities with European values.

The monsters who ran the USSR, after their violent revolution against the old guard, were intellectuals. Every one of those people, including Stalin—who was not only a student in his youth, but also a religious seminary student—had no difficulty in ordering mass murders, creating artificial famines, and imprisoning thousands of innocent people in Siberia. This was all done, supposedly, for the idea of a blissful Marxist paradise at some point in the future.

An old joke goes: "There is pie in the sky when you die by and by," meant to encourage people to feats of sacrifice today for paradise tomorrow.

Hitler's pie, of course, would be a world free of Jews, Gypsies, Slavs, Blacks, and Asians. The Nazis would preside over a world of blue-eyed blonds who would revive the (imagined) Aryan religions of their ancestors and dance naked in fields of wildflowers.

Stalin's pie was "the withering away of the state." In theory, communists would take over the world and all things would be shared equally. Of course, it would be a tomorrow that would be far away. Soviet intellectuals never seemed to notice that the state did not wither away.

Intellectuals in Serbia during the 1980s and 90s, some of their best and brightest, came up with the notion that it was time for ethnic cleansing. A 400-year-old ethnic quarrel would be settled by a quick genocide (which they contemplated) and then there would be pie in the sky.

Intellectuals in Rwanda designed a very modern program for carrying out genocide by using the state media to stir up the ignorant. The genocide was carried out with what they had at hand: machetes. This was indeed a mixture of old and new for dreadful ends.

Pol Pot, Cambodia's leader during the 1970s, was an intellectual who had been educated in France. Yet he came up with a piece of primitivism—the idea of returning the country to its "virtuous" agrarian roots—that propelled a genocide of as many urban and educated Cambodians as his thugs could find. One-third of the population was either exterminated or driven abroad.

China's Mao was an intellectual too, and some of his ideas were so terrible that millions of Chinese died from them. He ruined systems that worked (Chinese agriculture) and tried instead collectivism, which resulted in famine. He stirred up intellectuals (students and teachers) to sally forth and kill other intellectuals in the name of his "cultural revolution," a folly that set back China's development by a decade or more. It also devastated a generation of Chinese intellectuals.

Another horror out of current news was the conviction in Belgium of four Rwandans for murder in the 1994 Hutu genocide against Tutsis, all citizens of the same country. (The Belgian trials are distinct from the UN Tribunal trying war crimes related to this genocide.) That the four defendants include two well-educated Catholic nuns, a National University professor, and a presidential aide, adds to the horror. With the nuns, not even religious thinking, let alone intellect, interfered with their savagery.

One of the nuns provided gasoline to torch a building housing 500 Tutsis who had sought sanctuary. The other nun forced hundreds of Tutsis hiding in her convent to leave. Six hundred died, and she then asked the mob to remove the last thirty Tutsis hiding, who were then also slaughtered. The professor personally murdered at least seven Tutsis, including a colleague and his colleague's wife. The presidential aide incited Hutus to murder Tutsis in the now infamous radio broadcasts. [*SFC*, 4/18/01]

These are some of the reasons for looking twice at intellectuals, but it is not necessarily the reason for the twisted thinking of religious fanatics who are hostile to everything in the modern world, except for what they can use to attain and keep control.

The ultimate horror was the attack on America on 9/11/01, carried out by men from middle-class, educated families, in the name of a primitive perversion of Islam.

Religious twisted thinking

There is another reason for the recent emergence of the once marginalized religious "one-notes" around the world. Many, if not most, of these people are not intellectuals. They claim to get their thoughts and values directly from their notion of God and their religions, and their thinking processes are highly selective.

The ultra-religious of all sects share one value system: they detest the secular world with all its choices and all its freedoms, particularly freedom for a sector of society that has never been free before; i.e., women.

They also abhor the inevitable other side of freedom, which is license, and in this they have a point. However, it is a basic religious tenet that the Creator gave us free will to choose good or evil. The nature of this gift is that one does not have freedom without the possibility of abusing that freedom. [Farhat-Holzman, *Strange Birds*]

It is a hateful thought to Islamist clerics that women should have freedoms such as those of men. "They should be completely free," said a Pakistani cleric, "only within four walls." [*SFC*, 12/25/00]

"There should be freedom of thought," said an Egyptian cleric, "unless the thought is insulting to Islam." [*CSM*, 1/29/01]

"There should be freedom for one to convert to Islam," said the chief Afghan cleric, "but if one chooses to leave Islam, he should be put to death." [*SFC*, 1/ /01]

The Taliban in Afghanistan, of course, put this notion into practice. In August of 2001, a humanitarian aid agency that has been providing clothing, tents, and food to desperate Afghanis was raided and shut down by the Taliban because it was accused of conducting clandestine missionary efforts. The Christian aid workers were lucky to get out with their lives. Afghan converts were not so lucky. What the Taliban really wanted was freedom for the top dogs to do what they saw fit, and no freedom for anyone else.

Religion, from the beginning of state organization of this powerful institution, has never been an advocate of freedom. To obtain the benevolence of the deity or deities, priests were compelled to carry out rituals exactly as dictated by some ancient shaman (or prophet).

Someone at the beginnings of Mesoamerican culture declared that the sun would not come up if the Sun God were not fed a diet of human hearts. Until the Spaniards put an end to this nonsense, no one had the courage to put it to the test.

Karen Armstrong writes about one ultra-Orthodox sect in Israel that professes the belief that it is only their ceaseless devotion to prayer and reading the Torah that keeps God from destroying the world. They too have not put it to the test. [Armstrong, 208]

A curious thing about religious thinking is that it can interpret events in two antithetical ways. When things are good, the religious authorities can claim it is because of their pious rituals. However, when things are bad, they can claim that someone has offended the gods and that person must be sought out and punished. The story of Oedipus in Greek mythology has the shaman accounting for a plague by the actions of the king, who (albeit unknowingly) had killed his father and married his mother.

The Bible fingers King David as the culprit who had offended God and thereby caused the plague in Jerusalem. He had taken to wife a woman married to another man whom he managed to eliminate by sending him into the front lines of a war. God punished David twice: by bringing on the plague and by killing the first baby born out of this questionable relationship.

Among the Zulu in the nineteenth century, certain priests were designated as "sniffers" who could sniff out witches and traitors whom they could then torture to death for "the general good." (Sadly, this is still going on in rural South Africa.) [*CSM*, 12/6/00]

When the Black Plague struck Europe, local clerics preached that it was God's wrath that Jews had not been converted to Christianity. They also accused the Jews of poisoning wells. This second charge was self-fulfilling when murderous mobs threw the corpses of thousands of Jews into the wells. [The book to see is *Constantine's Sword,* by James Carroll, 2001.]

Eventually, however, even the creative twisted thinking of the clerics runs dry when there are no more scapegoats to blame. At that point, the common people sometimes turn their anger on the religion, the priests, and the gods who no longer protect them.

The ancient gods of the Roman Empire could not stand up to the famine, plagues, and barbarian invasions that followed a violent climatic event in the sixth century AD. [Keys, 172] Christianity with its promise of rewards after this life had more to offer than paganism to the beset people of that century. The old religions lost out.

There is evidence of violent religious revolution in Mesoamerica during that same period. Prolonged drought, famine, and plague created such major havoc that the common people turned on their priests and rulers. Archeologists have found evidence of a violent massacre of aristocrats and priests whose bodies were torn limb from limb, along with the statuary representing the former gods. [Keys, 193]

During the horrors of the fifteenth-century Spanish Inquisition and later persecutions of Jews throughout Europe in the seventeenth century, many Jews lost their faith in the god of their ancestors and converted to Christianity—not out of belief, but out of despair. [Armstrong, 7]

The same despair caused many Jews who suffered the Nazi holocaust to abandon belief. "How could a "Just God" permit such a horror?" they asked. Religion has always had difficulty in accounting for evil as a creation of a just god.

Despite defections from religion by people traumatized by evil, the modern revealed religions (Judaism, Christianity, and Islam) have an answer for their long-suffering followers: God's Will. It is difficult to argue this position with a true believer, but it seems to me to fall into the category of "pie in the sky when you die by and by." No one has returned from the sky to tell us whether there is pie or not.

One ultra-Orthodox rabbi in Israel came out with an explanation for the Holocaust that left rational Jews dumbfounded. He claimed that the Nazi Holocaust was God's punishment of Jews for sins in their past lives (since when did Jews believe in reincarnation?) and for their abandonment of Orthodox practices. [*SFC*, 8/6/00]

The Christian Right spokesmen Jerry Falwell and Pat Robertson set off a similar firestorm among Americans reeling from the terrorist attacks on New York and Washington, on September 11, 2001. They asserted that an angry God had allowed the terrorists to succeed in their deadly mission because the US had become a nation of abortion, homosexuality, secular schools and courts, and the American Civil Liberties Union. [*SCS*, 9/15/01]

Intellectuals gone religious

It is difficult to ascertain if certain foreign students from religious backgrounds who receive Western educations ever accepted the values of Western humanism. Did they reject the West after understanding it—or did they not try to understand it? Was their educational experience more for prestige than for learning how to think critically?

For many students, getting a degree from a recognized institution is a union card for rising to a position of power in their homeland. It is a standing joke in the Muslim world that a medical degree is a ticket to a political career, not a medical career. Perhaps it is time to look at medical education.

We have already touched upon medical doctors who discarded the basic tenet of medicine—do no harm—and became subsumed in the cult of Hitler or, in the case of the Japanese, the cult of the Emperor. We have a further example in the practicing cardiac surgeon Ikuo Hayashi, who became the mad scientist of the Japanese Shri Shinrikyo cult that set off sarin nerve gas in the Tokyo subways. [Lifton, 143] Were these doctors merely medical technologists who had no humanities education at all?

There may be a problem with science education altogether. It is so difficult and demanding to go through the engineering curriculum that there seems to be little room for philosophy, literature, or history—disciplines that hone critical thinking. At least in the West, such materials are offered in the better high schools or college preparatory academies, as well as in the countless small colleges that excel in general education teaching.

What happens to students who come from cultures where students learn to memorize and never to question? They may, on the basis of their school grades or family money, gain entrance into Western universities, but they may always have difficulty with critical thinking.

There is no question about the native intelligence of university students, no matter where they are from. There is only a question about how those minds are used, and the evidence is discouraging. There are myriad examples, both domestic and international.

One domestic example is Jeffrey Schilling, a 25-year-old Oakland, California, native who had the benefit of an education that included Exeter Academy, his prep school, and Massachusetts Institute of Technology. [*SFC*, 4/14/01]

This starry-eyed romantic became a convert to Islam through a computer romance with a Philippine Muslim woman. He married her and went to the Philippines to show himself sympathetic to the long-simmering Muslim guerrilla war against the Philippine government. He walked right into a camp of Muslim kidnappers for ransom, a group whose leader, Abu Sayyaf, had been trained in Afghanistan.

Schilling's purpose was to debate theology with this man, whose cousin just happened to be Jeffrey Schilling's wife. Shilling was taken captive and held for ransom for seven miserable and frightening months, until rescued by the Philippine government.

Along with losing 100 pounds while in captivity, he seems to have lost his stupidity also. He now hopes to see that band of cutthroats wiped out, he says, and nobody has asked how he feels about his new religion.

Chip Johnson, a *San Francisco Chronicle* columnist who covered Schilling's release, noted: "At least it has to be a revelation for a Californian to learn that he is likely to have more in common with an Iowa farmer than his philosophical comrade-in-arms locked in the international struggle against government-sponsored oppression." [*SFC*, 4/14/ 2001]

Let us examine the mental processes of students who come from everywhere in the world to study in Western institutions. One of the more interesting examples of this is a cleric in Sudan, Hassan Turabi, who received a Cambridge education and then returned to his homeland where he became the power behind the dictatorship. He served as speaker of the parliament and as Sudan's chief Islamic theologian, and was said to be the architect of the draconian program to Islamize Sudan's south, which is largely Black, Christian, or Animist.

Turabi pushed for a strict Islamic state for Sudan's Muslims. Not only did he argue against any of the human rights notions of the West, but even urged that those Sudanese who were not Muslim must be forced to convert. This idea has spawned the ugliest and longest civil war imaginable, with the smell of racism, genocide, and slavery hanging over it. What did this man learn at Cambridge?

Apparently he learned something because on February 21, 2001, he was arrested for "conspiring with the southern rebels to topple the government." [*SFC*, 2/22/01] It took some time, but he was finally aware of the unforeseen consequences of his movement and wanted to put a stop to the horrors. Now he may be martyred.

Osama bin Laden, fugitive terrorist and religious fanatic who is wanted for prosecution by the United States and Saudi Arabia, also received a Western-style education. He is one of fifty-plus children of a very wealthy Yemeni father, and, as such, was the recipient of as good an education as money could buy. It seems that his entire education was turned on its head when he went on to university in Saudi Arabia, where he was heavily indoctrinated in Wahhabi fanaticism, training that obviously shaped this monster, who has decided that all "infidels" should die.

On Tuesday, September 11, 2001, he demonstrated that he has the means to do extraordinary damage. His agents were willing to commit suicide and mass murder with hijacked airliners used as missiles against American installations. The World Trade Center in New York was leveled and the Pentagon headquarters of the US Defense Department severely damaged, resulting in about 3,000 deaths.

Before this enormous exercise, his men had destroyed two US embassies in Africa in one day, and then attacked a US naval vessel refueling in Yemen.

According to evidence presented in the US federal trial of some of the foot soldiers of bin Laden, this man pointed to the exact places in pictures of two American embassies in east Africa where car bombs were to be detonated. He gloried in the idea of such death and destruction to show America what he thought of it. He also told his henchmen not to worry about civilian deaths because they did not matter in the holy war they were waging.

There is no doubt that his followers, most of whom cannot be said to have anything resembling an education that fosters critical thinking, find him to be dazzling. But his days are now numbered. The United States has driven him out of Afghanistan and he is hiding somewhere in Pakistan. He will not flourish.

Even the Jewish ultra-Orthodox have had a leader with secular education who cast it all aside for his vision of truth. The Seventh Rebbe of the Lubavitch Hasidic community, the late Menachem Mendel Schneerson (1904–94) had received a secular education. He had studied Jewish philosophy in Berlin and marine engineering at the Sorbonne. He came to the US in 1941 and married the daughter of the Sixth Rebbe, after which he abandoned his secular job with the US Navy and set about organizing Hasidim to convince Jews to come back to the fold. He sent out thousands of young Lubavitch males and females to found Habad houses where Jews could drop in and learn more about their sort of Judaism. They recruited in universities and on the streets of America with considerable success. [Armstrong, 213]

What is fascinating and puzzling about Rabbi Schneerson was his ability to understand modern science yet interpret the Bible literally: the world had been created by God in six days less than six thousand years ago.

He certainly knew how to use modern media for his purposes. At the time of his death, his followers were convinced he was the Messiah so long awaited (something he cleverly neither affirmed nor denied) and that his death would be followed by miracles and the end of time. It was not, but his followers are not deterred by facts; they are still waiting.

Finally, there were three news items, clustered within a week, that illustrated unbelievably stupid, if not twisted thinking. From Malaysia came the first. The article did not indicate the educational level of the perpetrators, but it certainly indicated stupidity. Three men were indicted for the murder of the American wife of a Malaysian. She was "ritually sacrificed" almost two years prior so that the murderers could get winning lottery numbers from the "spirits." Her body was just found and the men arrested for her murder. [*SFC*, 7/28/1]

The second report came from India. [*SFC*, 8/7/01] A mental asylum had burned to the ground with most of its patients chained to their beds. The bedlam had belonged to a Muslim shrine. The shrine's keepers believe (in this day and age) that mental patients are possessed by demons so they must be chained and abused.

The third was an article about a growing tide of circumcision deaths of young men in Africa caused by inept surgery, gross infections, and utter ignorance. [*SFC*, 8/6/01] Nobody is keeping track of the suffering and deaths of little girls and adolescent females who are treated to equally inept surgeries. This surgery is not circumcision, although its apologists use that term, but is Female Genital Mutilation, designed to do maximum damage to female sexuality so that girls will be controllable and married women faithful to their husbands. How twisted were the minds that dreamt up such ways to control children's sexuality, and all under religion!

Education with agendas

The idea of a university is very old. The word "university" promises universal knowledge, or optimistically, the best that the human mind has produced.

The most famous ancient library, of course, was the one in Alexandria that was burnt to the ground in antiquity. The next "university" library that we know of was established by the Shahs of the Persian Empire, some time between 300 and 600 AD. This university was housed in a town called Jundishapur, and its nexus was a library (largely medical) in which Greek, Persian, Syrian, Jewish, and Indian texts and ideas intermingled and were translated into Persian. [Bernard Lewis, ed., *The World of Islam*, "The Scientific Enterprise," 183]

After the Arabs conquered Persia in 631 CE and converted it to Islam, the new rulers became interested in this library, and Persians set to work translating everything into Arabic. This scholarly work fueled what was to become the great Golden Age of Islam, a period in which the great ideas and beginnings of science from ancient Greece and Rome were revived and augmented greatly by Muslim scholarship, which in turn, spurred Europe's renaissance of learning.

Both in the Muslim world and in the Christian European world, the idea of secular universal learning had fierce opposition. As long as times were good and there was money in the coffers and trade flowed well, the universities were supported. When plagues hit and the Mongols rolled in from Central Asia, the religious fanatics prevailed. They were able to point to these disasters as God's displeasure with people thinking of anything but prayer.

In addition to institutions of universal learning, there have always been institutions of religious learning. These still exist with certain societal modifications. Christian fundamentalist universities such as Bob Jones University and such Mormon universities as Brigham Young do offer the full range of secular learning but they augment it with strong emphasis on their own particular religious views of the universe. Their particular "holy books" can, when necessary, trump secular views.

Ultra-Orthodox Jewish yeshivas do not even pretend to offer "universal" learning. The only material thought fit for the mind is study of the Torah. It is the same in a whole system of Islamic institutions, ranging from the school in Qom, Iran, that produced the Ayatollah Khomeini to a system of "Jihad Universities" devoted to terrorist training in Pakistan and Yemen.

Ultra-Orthodox yeshivas

The Jewish ultra-Orthodox yeshivas (religious schools) began in the seventeenth century in the Jewish communities living in precarious isolation in the most backward parts of the Russian Empire and in Eastern Europe.

As the European enlightenment unfolded in the eighteenth century, the enforced isolation of Jews was ending and many joined the secular world and attended Western universities. Others, however, feared that this movement would spell the end of Judaism and they withdrew bitterly into separation and isolation from what they perceived as the "godless" world outside.

In 1803, a Lithuanian rabbi, Hayyim Volozhiner, founded the first of the yeshivas that differed radically from the old system of students coming to the synagogue to read the Torah and Talmud. It established a rigorous system of rote learning, preparation, and lively discussion (with conclusions already predetermined) that attracted bright young Jewish students from all over Europe.

Karen Armstrong notes that, "The young men were isolated in a quasi-monastic community, their spiritual and intellectual lives entirely shaped by the yeshiva. They were separated from their families and friends and immersed wholly in the world of Jewish scholarship." [Armstrong, 110] Secular knowledge was discouraged.

She further notes that all such embattled fundamentalist institutions were not fighting an outside enemy, such as the Gentile world, but rather internal enemies—other Jews who were not thinking as they were. We see this same thing in today's Islamic fundamentalism; it purports to oppose the modern world, but it fights viciously against other kinds of Muslims. In Pakistan, this has already reached the proportions of a civil war.

The Hasidic movement that started in Russia centuries ago as a reaction against the sterile study of the Torah without understanding the spiritual joy of Judaism was transformed in 1893 by the fifth in a dynasty of Lubavitch rabbis. He established a Habad Yeshiva that would create a cadre of young men to fight "the enemies of the Lord." The enemies, of course, were other Jews— Zionists, socialists, secular Jews— who must be fought so that the Messiah would come. [Armstrong, 148]

Today in Israel the battle between concepts of Judaism rages on. The "true Haredim" (ultra-Orthodox trembling ones) have become militantly segregationist. They believe that every detail of the lives of the faithful has cosmic importance. "Matters of dress, methods of study, even the cut of the beard, must be absolutely correct. ...Care should be taken that the right lapel overlaps the left, so that the right hand of the Most High, 'the right hand of the Lord uplifted,' in its exalted Love, predominates over the left side, which represents Power, the strength of the Evil Impulse." [Armstrong, 204]

It is astonishing to know that while these anti-Zionist Haredim are only a small minority—only 20,000 in Israel and several tens of thousands in the United States—their influence is out of proportion. In Israel, for political reasons having to do with a multi-party system, these people have political clout far beyond their numbers. There is a growing concern that these sects may eventually also achieve numbers because of the huge families they encouraged.

In the United States, the recent presidential pardon of four ultra-Orthodox criminals in a New York Hasidic village (who received large government funds for a nonexistent school) has angered many people. One wonders why they have such political pull. In another similar case in San Francisco of an ultra-Orthodox rabbi, an embezzler, the judge was entreated to release the criminal because he was indispensable to his ultra-Orthodox community.

What do these ultra-Orthodox schools teach and how does this constitute "education?" In these yeshivas, Jews do not study to acquire information that could later be put to practical use. Instead, they study the Torah so rigorously that even such topics as obsolete temple animal sacrifice rituals and obsolete tort law absorb years of study involving intense discussion with their teachers because these were supposedly God's laws. [Armstrong, 211]

Muslim fundamentalist institutions

The first time the West encountered these Jihad U's was when we heard about "students" in Afghanistan who were taking control of the country and putting an end to the interminable factional fighting. My first thought was that these were university students and that perhaps they would bring some light to the darkness. Alas, it was not so.

These "students" were the Taliban, a faction of very ignorant and largely illiterate foot soldiers led by old fanatics who were custodians of their own peculiar interpretation of Islam. Along with guerrilla training, these students memorized the Koran in Arabic, not really understanding a word of it, but accepting the interpretation of their teachers. This scarcely passes for education, and the word "students" has long been dropped by the Western news media.

Two intrepid American journalists (see Chapter 3, Religious Fascism) traveled to Pakistan to explore these Jihad Universities first hand.

Robert Kaplan, an experienced journalist and global observer who has taken on some very unpleasant places around the world, such as Africa and the Balkans, has added the Pakistan/Afghanistan frontier to his travels. [*The Atlantic Monthly*, 9/2000]

Kaplan explored the tribal lands of this Afghan-Pakistan border and Indian subcontinent, along with the dark side of globalization. Baluchistan, a desperately poor and illiterate province peopled by the Baluchi tribe, is divided between Iran and Pakistan. On the Pakistani side, the province is awash in murders, kidnappings, and a revolutionary "Pashtoon National People's Party" who want an independent Pashtoonistan.

Kaplan has noted what no officials have yet acknowledged: that Pakistan and Afghanistan have become a single unit, for all practical purposes. This is deadly for Pakistan. [Kaplan, 69]. The so-called schools that he visited were nothing more than training camps for future killers.

Jeffrey Goldberg, a second American journalist who toured the Pakistan/Afghan border, specifically visited madrasas to learn about the "education" of a holy warrior. [*The New York Times Magazine*, 6/25/00: "Inside Jihad U."]

In a Pakistani religious school called the Haqqania Madrasa, Osama bin Laden was a hero, the former Taliban's leaders were famous alumni, and the next generation of mujahedeen was still being militantly groomed. Goldberg made this observation after he was permitted to attend "classes" and the students seemed happy to talk to him after they decided he was "all right." [Goldberg, 32] Even after all their brainwashing about how evil Americans are and even more so when Jewish, they could not reconcile the hateful description with this seemingly nice fellow.

What the students most wanted to talk about was sex, since in this environment in which there was not even a grandmother, not to mention younger women, they were sex-obsessed. He was asked whether American men were allowed by law to keep boyfriends and girlfriends at the same time, which says something about their own sexual standards.

The students sat with their teacher on the floor for four to eight hours a day. The teacher read in Arabic, and the students imitated, which was all they could do since they did not understand a word of it.

But understanding or not, this school "graduated" more leaders of the Afghan Taliban than any other school in the world, including those in Afghanistan. With no world history, no math, science, or computer labs, it is difficult to think of this school as comparable to what is generally considered to be education in today's world. Rather, it is a training ground for jihad, or holy war.

In practical terms, the jihad is war against other less fanatical Afghan factions, against India in the endless Kashmir struggle, and against Russians in Chechnya. But in theory (certainly in the classroom), the jihad is against Americans and the "Zionist Entity," Israel.

The students said they would love to use nuclear bombs against Israel, and they all loved Osama bin Laden and wanted to be like him.

From the explosion of the Taliban upon the scene in Afghanistan, they committed acts that have given an undeservedly bad name to the Prophet Mohammad, whose religion they professed to support. In 1994, when the "students" marched on Kabul, they closed down all girls' schools, fired female doctors, murdered homosexuals, and staged public amputations. [Goldberg, 53]

Their most incredible stupidities included the destruction of pre-Islamic Buddhist art treasures and the demand that non-Muslims in Afghanistan wear distinctive clothing so that they could be readily identified (shades of the Nazi yellow stars for Jews). This measure, of course, drove out the essential community of Hindu Indian merchants, which increased the poverty of Afghanistan.

Then this backwater of benighted thinking gave sanctuary to the global terrorist network led by Osama bin Laden, which launched an attack on two symbols of American power: the New York World Trade Center and the US Department of Defense headquarters at the Pentagon. This was twisted thinking.

Once more, religious ideology has spawned war. The book to read on this topic is *On the Causes of War* by Michael Andregg, Ground Zero Minnesota, Minneapolis, 1999.

Thank you, O Lord, for not making me a woman.
—Orthodox Hebrew daily prayer for men

Chapter 7.
A simmering problem around the religious world: Women

Feminists already know that conservative religion is not their friend. Primitive fear of women's blood and both envy and disgust at their ability to bring forth new life would have disappeared long ago had religion not enshrined them. From Plato to John Stewart Mill, there have been wise men who *suspected*, at least, that if opportunities were equal, women might be little different from men.

However, there have been few such wise men, and their voices were as wind in the wilderness, drowned out by the thunder of every mainstream religion in the world, not to mention every primitive society from which religions derive.

By custom, from ancient times women were property, and not to be thought of as fellow humans, no matter what their own religion's prophets might have said on the subject. They were, as childbearers, the key to the next generation of property—children—and both were needed as unpaid labor.

Without women and children under firm control, there would be no continuity of community and no guarantee of a religious community. Furthermore, religious community leaders have enough problems with men who want to think for themselves; they did not want problems with women too. Thoroughly indoctrinated women have always been the bedrock of maintaining traditional values into the next generation.

In most religious societies, women have been kept from from literacy and education and from leadership roles from the beginning of the advent of agriculture. The ancient *de facto* slavery of women was now blessed by the God of the Universe.

Although the blame for women's status may be laid at the feet of organized religions, it would be unfair to blame this on the world's great religious prophets. Zoroaster's first convert was a queen; Moses was saved by his sister and the Pharaoh's daughter; the Buddha was rescued from a fast that nearly killed him by a little girl; Jesus shocked his male followers by his kindness and equal treatment of women; and Mohammad's first convert was his wife. Each of them treated women far better than their followers did.

For a woman to defy tradition and her family's hold over her to follow a new prophet requires enormous sacrifice. Women were the earliest martyrs, as well as the earliest disciples of new religions. Yet once the religion was on its feet and the Prophet gone, the older traditional attitudes came back.

Consider the difference between the attitude of Jesus toward his women followers and that of St. Paul, who admonished women not to speak in church. Or consider the role of strong women in the Hebrew Bible, including such wise women as the Judge, Deborah. Why were there no such women in the Jewish Diaspora and why do the ultra-Orthodox in Israel proclaim that God does not like women's voices—or women judges?

In Islam, the reverence of the Prophet Mohammad toward his businesswoman wife and his love and respect for the wives he accumulated after his first wife's death are documented. [Armstrong: Muhammad, 79] His youngest wife led an army in battle and preached to the congregation in the mosque. Yet his supposedly devout followers among today's Islamists want women to be invisible, silent, and under lock and key.

I hope it is clear, then, that I am not attacking the founders of the world's great religions as the source of religious persecution and suppression of women. Nonetheless, the institutions that followed these prophets are to blame. Religions take on a life of their own, and for all the steps forward in morality and ethics that come with each new religion, dreadful cultural behaviors return and somehow become enshrined. [Farhat-Holzman, *Strange Birds from Zoroaster's Nest*]

Hateful attitudes toward women are universal and timeless, as illustrated by the following sayings, compiled by the United Nations before the 1995 Women's Conference in Beijing:

The Chinese, until the Communist Revolution, had the following attitudes enshrined in proverbs:

> *We keep a dog to watch the house;*
> *A pig is useful too.*
> *We keep a cat to catch a mouse;*
> *But what can we do*
> *With a girl like you?*

> *Eighteen goddess-like daughters are not equal to one son*
> *with a hump.*

> *Such is the stupidity of woman's character that it is incum-*
> *bent upon her to distrust herself and obey her husband.*
> — Confucius, 500 BC

And from the ancient Hebrews, we have:

> *In law...a hundred women are equal to only one [male] witness.*
> —Talmud, Yebamot 88B

From more modern sources, we have:

> *Eloquence in women shouldn't be praised; it is more fit-*
> *ting for them to lisp and stammer.*
> —Martin Luther, 1538 AD

> *Nature intended women to be our slaves.*
> —Napoleon, 1817 AD

> *Do you know why God created women? Because sheep can't type.*
> —Texas State Sen. Kenneth Armbruster, 1970

*Women cannot compete with men in the rational sciences
and problems of pure logic. Abstaining from housework
is dreadful torture for a woman.*
—Hadi Khameini, Iran, 1993

*Women cannot serve in the trenches of war because they have
their monthly periods which makes them get infections.*
—Newt Gingrich, 1995
(What on earth did this university professor and US
congressman mean by this? Did he actually consider
menstruating women infection prone?)

The following proverbs reflect attitudes around the world to the
birth of a girl child:

Water spilled on the ground.
—Taiwan

Prostitutes to be exchanged for cattle at the time of marriage.
—Uganda

Maggots in the rice.
—China

Only weeds.
—Zulus of South Africa

*A girl lets you down twice: once at birth and the second
time when she marries.*
—Korea

These sayings are but the tip of the iceberg. There is a positive
hysteria among fundamentalist religions today toward women and
a passionate effort to prevent them from infiltrating modern secular
values into their societies.

The rhetoric against the modern world is aimed at what is perceived as the sexual promiscuity of women who are not otherwise constrained.

Attitudes toward women have been with us from primeval times, but the most influential models are exemplified by ancient Greece and Rome. The Greek model gave us the idea of seclusion: keep women locked up and veiled so that they will not be able to disgrace their families. This model was picked up by the Persian Empire, the Chinese, Indian, and the Muslim worlds—and independently by the Inca nobility.

In Rome, ladies were reared to have internal controls to protect their virtue. They were expected to resist temptations and to be virtuous because of their character. This model was absorbed by Western Europe and the modern secular world.

There were great Greek women who were companions to their men—the famous Aspasia who was the mistress of Pericles, for example. However, such women were not "ladies," that is, were neither the wives of respectable men nor the mothers of their children. A woman had the choice of mental stimulation or motherhood, never both.

Around the world today, women are subjected to violent, demeaning treatment that the perpetrators insist is religiously ordained. As women slowly become literate, they are reading their religious texts and finding many of these interpretations without foundation. Even when the texts warrant violence (as instructions in the Koran about when a husband may "lightly" beat a stubborn wife), literate women are challenging the continuation of such behavior.

Not only have the age-long habits of abuse of women continued into the modern period, there seems to be a worsening of this behavior. In Bangladesh, for example, there has been an explosion of cases of men throwing acid in the faces of young women who refuse their advances. The men, even when imprisoned, see nothing wrong with what they have done. It is their right, they say. [*SFC*, 11/17/2000]

Elsewhere in the world, there is evidence of increasing male fury at the standards of modernization—only where women are concerned. These same men are perfectly happy with modern tools, automobiles, weapons, computers, radios, and televisions, but bristle at the idea of women having any freedom of choice in their lives.

It seems that in the more miserable cultures around the world, those that are going through painful transitions and gross population explosions, men are reluctant to give up their one remaining power: power over women.

When experienced world traveler V.S. Naipal explored the resurgence of Islamic fundamentalism after the successful Islamic Revolution in Iran, he visited countries from Iran through Indonesia and found the same phenomenon: men who were overjoyed that women were being "put back in their place." This was a ubiquitous response, and surprised Naipal with its vehemence. [Naipal, *Among the Believers*]

The hostility toward women may well be a backlash against the emancipation of women in more developed societies. The rage and anger expressed by traditional men is based on a misguided belief that emancipated women are "prostitutes." Thus the choice for women is between being traditional (under lock and key) or being seen as prostitutes (free to make what these men are certain must always be bad choices).

It is also possible that until recently no one attempted to document the extent of violence against women because violence was the norm. Perhaps the numbers seem so horrific because we are only now trying to count (no easy task). It is not possible to know whether there has been an increase in violence against women without a baseline; all we can tell is that there seems to be an increase in overt rage.

Religion, or rather very twisted interpretations of religion, plays an enormous role in validating the suppression and abuse of women around the world. At the moment, the worst cases can be found among ultra-conservative Muslims, followed by Neo-Nationalist Hindus, conservative Christians, and ultra-Orthodox Jews. The tradition of wife abuse is also strong among tribal communities—in Polynesia, Africa, New Guinea, and Australia— whose members were, until recently, polytheists or animists, but may now be Christian or Muslim. The "Noble Savage" is a myth.

Islam

The worst example of abuse of women in the Muslim world was Taliban Afghanistan. The Taliban rulers of Afghanistan were the victors in Afghanistan's tribal civil wars, and they succeeded by passing themselves off as "students" with a severe but righteous version of Islamic justice. They professed their intention to stop the incessant rape and looting that accompanied the factional tribal power struggles.

The term "students" (Talab) refers to religious students, not university students as the Western press initially assumed. These students, as described earlier in this book, memorize the Koran in Arabic, which is not their language, and take their interpretations of Islam from their leaders.

The flood of information that came out of Afghanistan then was a daily chronicle of horrors. The Afghan Taliban's supreme religious leader, Mullah Mohammed Omar, destroyed an art treasure of early Buddhist sculpture because it "insulted Islam." When such pronouncements were met by a roar of outrage by the outside world, the Taliban were astonished, just as they were when their attitudes toward women were protested. It may well be that they are just more ignorant than malicious. [*SFC*, 2/27/01] Despite the outrage, Mullah Omar ordered his Ministry of Vice and Virtue to send out the art destroyers, and the job was done.

The Taliban's next outrage was to demand that Hindu merchants living in Afghanistan identify themselves by wearing yellow ribbons pinned to their clothing. This evoked the Nazis in Western minds.

An Iranian spokesman (not identified) [*SFC*, 3/1/01] was bemused by such stupid pronouncements from what passes for clergy in Afghanistan. Iranians appear enlightened in comparison.

Until the above incident, most of the Taliban's bile was heaped on Afghan women. They deprived professional women of their work (which has left the country with a dearth of school teachers, bureaucrats, doctors, and secular judges). A draconian dress code for women was enforced that required total invisibility (head-to-toe coverage, including even eyes) and total inaudibility (rubber-soled shoes so that they cannot be heard walking). Women were not allowed to leave home unless accompanied by a male relative. The Taliban also required all lower-storey windows to be painted over so that no one can look into a house from the street. All girls' schools were closed.

All of this was justified as necessary for the safety for women; in fact, it displayed utter scorn. The authorities perhaps would have been very happy to do without women at all, other than as mothers of boy children, and one suspects that if they could have had boys without them, they would have.

Village women, who do a large part of the country's agricultural work, could not work in total coverup. They had never been required to observe such hijab before. The requirement certainly played (and still plays) a role in the shortage of food in Afghanistan.

As backward as Afghanistan had always been, it bumbled along. Under the Taliban, it approached total collapse. The country had lost its best men and women in an exodus of several million people who fled early. The last exodus before the American invasion appeared like a death march: starving peasants, mostly women and children, who could not gain admittance to even the meager Pakistani camps and who were starving and freezing to death on the roads out of Afghanistan.

The country's problems were a combination of natural disaster (drought) and man-made folly, and what made it more pitiful was that the Taliban had so alienated even the most forgiving outsiders (the UN and other aid agencies) that little help was forthcoming. The arrest of the employees of one Christian aid agency for the capital crime of pros-elytizing was vigorously protested by the UN. [*SFC*, 8/8/01]

The status of women is now beginning to improve—certainly in Kabul. Elsewhere in the country, however, change is slow.

Pakistan

Afghanistan's neighbor Pakistan is also teetering on the edge of collapse, and, once more, the leading cause is a form of Islam so back-ward and repressive that the country cannot thrive. The injection of conservative Islam into what began as a secular state has taken a dread-ful toll on what a modern country most needs: secular education.

There are still professional women in the urban areas of Pakistan, as there have been from the country's beginnings, and the lawyers among them have been waging a losing battle against the imposition of *Zinna*, or Islamic Women's Law.

Under Pakistan's notion of Islamic Law, a woman can only defend herself against charges of sexual impropriety by seeking four witnesses to vindicate her. This is a curious perversion of Islam considering that the Prophet Mohammad required two male witnesses before a woman could be condemned. In Pakistan, an accused woman may be jailed for years upon the accusation of her husband, or any other male witness, which also violates the Prophet's intent and words, if today's fanatics care.

Those women who are jailed for offenses against the women's purity laws are in urban areas only; in the tribal and rural areas of Pakistan, a perceived offender's fate is more likely murder at the hands of one of her blood relatives for "bringing shame on the family." Her fate is death even for running away from an abusive husband. There is no exit.

A combination of conservative Islam and the *de facto* observance of India's caste system have added to the country's problems. The educated and ruling caste of Pakistan has demonstrated little concern for public education, which is exacerbated by the faulty Islamic notion that women should not be educated. (The Prophet Mohammad did not advocate ignorance, it should be said.)

The result for Pakistan has been a population explosion, ecological degradation from too many people living on too little land, and a population too ignorant to dig itself out of this hole. Political life, certainly democratic political life, cannot flourish in a caste society in which the majority is ignorant, traditional, and economically depressed.

It is now a given that the greatest investment a backward country can make in its future is to educate its girls. Pakistan is not doing this at all.

Algeria

Many visitors to Algeria have spent most of their time in the coastal and French-influenced regions. When you speak French or English to sophisticated and educated people, stay in beautiful beach resorts, and eat the wonderful French-influenced foods, it can blind you to the less developed parts of the country. Algeria, under its lovely surface, has been a seething cauldron of resentment.

The struggle against France for independence was protracted and ugly. After independence, the ruling party reflected the spirit of the time: it was nationalist and socialist, and the purported aim of the rulers was to bring Algeria into the family of modern nations. That was the *zeitgeist* of post-World War II decolonization.

The spirit of hope promoted an enormous population explosion, which made it impossible for the government to keep up with the demand for education and for jobs. Besides, a government that remains in power too long loses touch and becomes corrupt.

When the authoritarian (and secular) military government finally yielded to the desire for an honest election, Algeria began to fall apart. The election was to be held in two phases: municipalities first and then national. The municipal election results horrified the secular state when they saw that the Islamic radicals (shades of Iran!) had made a sweep. The national election was quickly canceled and a vicious civil war broke out.

On one side were Islamic Fundamentalists who began assassinating police, journalists, and professional women. On the other side was a government that rounded up, jailed, and abused radical students (beards gave them away) and known Islamists.

The outside world had a dilemma. Conscientious liberals could not support a repressive government, but if they had any sense, they could not support Muslim factions that boasted that there would be one man, one vote, one time. (Religious fascists have a policy of winning by stealth.)

Eventually the government called another election, and this time a moderate government won the national contest. The majority of thinking Algerians recognize how close they came to losing everything if they had voted for the Islamic parties as a "protest vote,"—the reason Islamist parties did so well in the first round.

Despite what seems to have been a decent and fair election, the most radical of the Islamist parties went underground and they declared war on their perceived enemies. They have since been joined by a criminal underground that has been crossing the country as night riders, invading villages at night and leaving a trail of slaughter behind them. Women are the most frequent targets, being carried off to slavery, sexual abuse, and murder by the raiders.

In urban areas, women journalists, judges, university professors, and unveiled university students have been targeted for death or acid attacks. Even on "women-only" beaches, a concession to the fanatics, women have been attacked and decapitated for daring to expose their bodies.

The urban areas now seem to have been taken back by the authorities, but the mayhem continues unabated in the hinterland. The condition of rural women is precarious, and no one seems to know what to do to stop the madness.

Once more, we are seeing poisonous hatred against women: at first, against educated and modern women, but eventually just being female is enough. This has little support from traditional Islam, yet has enormous support from today's worst radicals posing as strict Muslims.

Egypt

Egypt has long prided itself on being the cultural nexus of Islamic modernization, which began in the 19th and early 20th centuries. Several generations of educated women emerged in Egypt, women who were not fighting Islam, but were fighting antiquated traditions posing as Muslim. They became professors, writers and artists, government officials, diplomats and scientists, and proud Egyptians. They were modern and unveiled.

Today these women, as mothers and grandmothers, are horrified to see their young women increasingly adopting Islamic veiling again. University professors have watched the occasional headscarf now become the dominant mode of dress. Is this youthful rebellion or misguided piety?

There is even a court case brought about by a young woman in one of Egypt's most modern and international universities who wants to wear an Afghan-style burqa that obscures even her eyes! The university administration is reluctant to permit such a thing because in such total coverup her identity cannot be determined. How will a professor know that she is his student, or that she is the person taking an exam? How will security-minded officials know that there is not a machine gun under that burka? In times such as these, this is an issue. [*CSM*, 1/17/01]

The liberal students at the university have taken up this young woman's cause as an issue of "civil liberty," a position that they will later regret when they all lose their civil liberties as Islamists take over.

Malaysia and Indonesia

Both of these countries were, until recently, rapidly modernizing and doing well economically. They comprise part of the "Asian Tigers," countries demonstrating phenomenal economic growth.

Simultaneous with what was beginning to be a viable and educated middle class in the urban areas, another phenomenon was taking place in the countryside: Islamization. There is always a lead/lag between rapid development in the cities and the countryside. Changes from tradition affect rural people the most. There was an exodus of youth to the cities to participate in the economic bonanza, and when these young people returned home, disillusioned that instant wealth was not forthcoming, the radicals were ready for them.

There has been a long-term effort funded by Saudi money to establish conservative Islamic schools in such places, providing scholarships for young men with leadership capability to continue their schooling in Arabia. These young men return to their countries and establish Islamic organizations aimed at taking power.

This program has fueled similar efforts in Nigeria and Pakistan. [Naipal, *Beyond Belief* and *Among the Believers*]. The evidence that such Islamic radicalization is happening is the profusion of head covering on women and girls. There comes a time when a female dare not defy this issue without risk to her life and safety.

Polygamy, which was going out of style under the assault of modern values, has returned, and even well educated and professional women are being sucked back into this dysfunctional system in Malaysia.

Indonesia, however, has confounded our alarm by holding several decent elections and the middle class has rallied to the modern, secular world. This is a hopeful note.

Turkey

When Kamal Ataturk established modern Turkey in the 1920s, he was convinced that the only way to transform Turkey's moribund culture was to educate everyone and uncouple religion from governance. Turkey is today the only Muslim country that is resolutely, and by constitution, secular. Iran's attempt to do the same failed (I think temporarily) when a revolution transformed a modernizing state into an Islamic Republic.

Turkey's problems stem from its demographic divide: the western half of the country is much more educated and prosperous than the eastern and traditional half, which has economic problems exacerbated by a high birthrate. Where conservative societies suppress women, particularly under the umbrella of religion, populations explode.

Exploding rural populations flow to the cities in hope of finding work and a better life than they have in the country. They are dislocated, their family and clan links broken, and it does not take long for these squatter communities to become resentful. The antiquated Turkish bureaucracy cannot handle the needs of these people adequately.

Where there is a vacuum, something rushes in to fill the void. Resurgent Islamic groups are finding easy pickings among the new urban unhappy. The same thing happened in Algeria, Iran (before 1978), Egypt, and Pakistan, and has proven very destabilizing for all these societies.

The only government taking on this issue is that of Turkey. Islam is not permitted to function politically in Turkey, and there are daily battles over this.

Of course, the most visible form of resurgent Islam is the head covering of women. The government is reinforcing the wall of separation between church and state in every instance that it can. Secular Turks constantly remind the public that women are free to do or wear whatever they choose *except* when they represent the government.

Students at government universities and high schools, and workers in government offices, are not permitted to wear headscarves because that would imply government support of Islam. A woman elected to Parliament challenged this rule and was ejected when she refused to remove the scarf. But the challenges are ongoing.

For secular Turks, it is a battle against time. A massive water project that has been thirty years in development is aimed at providing economic development for the dry and backward eastern half of Turkey. There is hope that irrigation and hydroelectric power from this project will bring the region gradually into the economic mainstream of Turkey.

It is hoped that economic development will raise the educational level of the people, reduce the birthrate to a more manageable level, and allow a genuine middle class to emerge. These are the only antidotes to religious fundamentalism and religious fascism.

Hinduism

The conditions for women in India depend upon whether they are born into the right caste (a system that is beginning to collapse under the assault of the modern world) and born in the right part of the subcontinent. Where tradition and both fundamentalist Hinduism and Islam flourish (in the country's north) women suffer. As in Pakistan, there is precious little public education available in the traditional regions, and almost none for women. This situation is being eroded by private efforts and UN programs, which are undercutting the feudal landowners.

In the educated areas of India, religion is not much of an issue, except for those most stubborn of traditional institutions, marriage and caste. Women are starting to enjoy the fruits of good education, and educated women rank high in the marriage market. However, there is a shortage of women in the marriage market today, and Hinduism is at fault.

One dreadful consequence of misguided Hinduism is the bias against girl children. Hindu Indian communities even living as far afield as Canada and the United States are using the technology of ultrasound to determine the gender of a fetus. This technology is generally followed by abortion of females, with a resultant drastic decline of female-to-male ratios among Indians.

The technology, of course, is only affordable by middle- to upper class Indians. We still hear that in rural India girl babies are frequently murdered at birth by the midwife or the mother herself at the insistence of the father.

All of this could be changed if the onerous custom of dowry payment to the husband's family could be made obsolete or illegal. In addition, an educated daughter is not the drag on the family that a traditional and ignorant daughter is. A secular Indian society could promote this.

Judaism

The majority of Jews living both in Israel and elsewhere around the world are moderate and largely secular. The changes that have come to women since the Industrial Revolution, the religious revolution of separation of church from state, and the political revolution of granting women equal political freedom with men, have brought Jewish women into the mainstream of modern society.

But, as Karen Armstrong notes in *The Battle For God,* in the periphery of Jewish life are pockets of passionate resistance to modern life. Ultra-Orthodox sects, both in Israel and in pockets in New York, Los Angeles, and a few in the American hinterland, try to live their lives in what they consider to be observant Judaism.

To them, observant means adherence to the Judaism of the long European Diaspora, particularly the style of life their ancestors led in villages in Lithuania, Poland, and Russia. They do not even have the historic hindsight to try to emulate Biblical Judaism, which ended when the Romans destroyed the last temple in 70 AD.

Their clothing is that of seventeenth-century Poland, not clothing of the ancient world. Their language is Yiddish, the common language of Jews in Europe, not Hebrew or the language of the country in which they are living. And their attitudes toward women are medieval.

Marriages are arranged, young women cloistered, and married women kept eternally pregnant and responsible for both household labor and outside work to support the noble male work of studying the Torah.

These groups, until recently, lived as invisibly as possible in the fringes of the world. They were swept up along with all the integrated Jews of Europe in Hitler's Final Solution death camps. Those few who survived the Holocaust restarted their communities in Israel and New York, and, thanks to their extremely high birthrates, their numbers and power have grown.

These communities appear to have material resources that are surprising, considering that the majority of men do nothing but devote their lives to "study" (only the Torah) and prayer. The resources for the communities in Israel come from the Israeli government in the form of welfare. The government also exempts the young men and women from the universal military service expected of the rest of the society.

The secular Israeli establishment, in founding the country, could not bring themselves to behave harshly to this Jewish remnant that had been so viciously persecuted in Europe. They yielded to them the exclusive right to determine Jewish law: family law (marriages and divorce), labor law (the Israeli airline cannot fly on the Sabbath), and dietary law (Kosher law must be observed in all state institutions). These concessions have created enormous inconvenience and resentment for the secular majority.

The emergence of Conservative and Reform Judaism in Western Europe and the United States gave Jews who wanted to join the cultural and political life of their countries an option. In Israel, there was no such choice until recently. Without recognizing Reform Judaism, one could be ultra-Orthodox or go without religion altogether; there was no middle way.

The nuisance of having ultra-Orthodox control over Israeli lives could be overlooked when Israelis were busy with life and death issues, such as survival. Recently, however, the ultra-Orthodox have become not only vocal, but also utterly offensive to the secular majority.

Women dressed in clothing suitable for Israel's Mediterranean climate are stoned and spat upon if they appear in ultra-Orthodox neighborhoods. People driving their automobiles on the Sabbath are stoned and threatened if they dare to appear in certain parts of Jerusalem.

An ultra-Orthodox assassin of former President Rabin was tried and sentenced by a woman judge. He vigorously objected to having a woman pass judgment over him. (He is in prison nonetheless.)

Women wishing to pray at the Wailing Wall have been assailed by bricks, chairs, and shouts of "whores!" from the increasingly bold fanatics. The Israeli Supreme Court finally ruled in favor of the women and has mandated police protection for them. [*SFC*, 5/12/00]

Visiting Conservative and Reform rabbis from the United States (with women rabbis among them) were verbally attacked by these same fanatics who deny any group but theirs the title of being Jewish.

The jokes and underground humor directed at the ultra-Orthodox bullies have turned to open resentment and questioning of the policy of government cosseting. Many people echo the thoughts of former Prime Minister Barak who questioned aloud the wisdom of continuing the exemption from the military and the excessive control of the ultra-Orthodox over Israeli institutions. Planes need to fly on Saturday. Tourists and many Israelis want food outside of Jewish dietary law. And farmers cannot afford to practice Biblical fallow laws that are inappropriate to modern life and economics. Revolt is in the air. [*SFC*, 9/18/00]

For all their bluster and new muscle, the ultra-Orthodox are having internal problems. In Israel, New York, and San Francisco, trusted elders have been proven masters of fraud and embezzlement (surely not the proper behavior of such religious gentlemen) and have been imprisoned for their crimes. The most notorious case recently is that of the four embezzlers and con men from a community in New York State who managed to gain pardons from former President Clinton.

For all their piety, such men see nothing wrong in robbing the government by embezzlement. They do not even seem to find anything wrong in fleecing their own ignorant and gullible followers. [*SFC*, 7/13/00]

Another problem is that despite all the brainwashing and bullying of children, who are told that if they do not obey they will go to hell (every fundamentalist group uses the same technique), increasing numbers of children are escaping and entering the secular world. In Israel, there are halfway houses to assist these youngsters to make the transition from the Middle Ages to the modern world.

So far, there are not many reports of girls escaping. It is much more difficult for young women, who are given little or no freedom, to even think of leaving family and community. But there is a growing movement to provide girls with some education, and with it lies some hope. Pious Jewish women are beginning to question why they have no voice in religion (only men make these judgments), and there must surely be some who are questioning the unremitting childbearing. The rank and file in ultra-Orthodox communities live in considerable poverty—the price for overpopulation and the exclusion of women from decision-making. The fat is in the fire.

Christianity

Pious Christianity has as bad a history with women as all other religions. Except for the earliest days of the new cult during Roman times, when women were major pillars of the young faith, their position has been subordinated.

Because of the ancient tradition of women being regarded as property, the new religion's power to change this was limited. Making divorce difficult, a novelty introduced by Christianity, gave women a modicum of protection against an arbitrary husband. However, despite

women are admonished to submit themselves to their husbands in all things. This pronouncement has subjected the fellowship to much good-humored criticism by the secular media, but also to the withdrawal of membership in this group by former President Jimmy Carter, who said that he could no longer count himself among the fellowship of the Southern Baptists.

Even worse are the extreme fringe cults, the Christian Aryans and the Christian Survivalists, as well as the Mormon Survivalists, who believe that they are saving humanity by holding fast to their male principles. Women are most assuredly in the back of the bus in such movements. The point is to restore men as masters—and these men mince no words in adding that in addition to gender superiority, they want racial superiority as well. These are ugly and often violent cults, and many are armed to the teeth.

Time and history are against such movements. Women are not going to return to slavery voluntarily, nor do most intelligent men want this. The secular world, which has provided freedom *from* religion, as well as freedom for religions to practice their faiths as long as they are not coercive, is in the mainstream of civilization.

However, we are in for a period of extremist backlash from groups that refuse to remain in the fringes of society. The confrontation of such groups with the educated mainstream can be helpful for all of us who need to be reminded that our freedoms must be defended. The wall between religion and the state must be kept solid. It protects religions from state interference on theological grounds, and protects all citizens from the horrors of religion with compulsion. Women in particular must be vigilant against religion stealing their human rights.

Alas, O Lord, to what a state dost Thou bring those who love Thee!
— St. Teresa of Avila, 1512–82

Chapter 8.
Associated issues: Population explosion, ecological degradation, or a cataclysm

Up to this point in our survey of resurgent and belligerent fundamentalist religion, we have looked at the mental processes of the players. However, religious hysteria is not just a psychological process in isolation. There are other triggers, man-made and earth-generated.

Some are the consequences of our animal nature, such as overpopulation and the ecological degradation that accompanies such explosions, including the frequent recurrence of plagues and warfare.

But other triggers come from the earth itself: volcanic eruptions that create years of climate change and cyclical climate changes that transform coastlines, agricultural regions, and drought and flood patterns.

How do these earthly things create religious hysteria? This takes us back to the origins of human religion itself, a mental construct based on fear.

Religion and order

Human societies appear to thrive on predictability. We go to great lengths to establish systems and patterns that repeat, giving us assurance of continuity. Religion claims to provide such assurance in its attempt to account for unforeseen disasters. Our Egyptian ancestors were concerned with the annual rising of the Nile, and much of their religious ritual was tied in with this natural event.

Astronomy

The Chinese and the Mayans watched the skies closely for omens and portents. The Chinese developed black powder to explode during eclipses to frighten off the dragon eating the sun or moon. It was only much later that this material was used to breech walls, and later still to propel cannonballs. The Mayans and their Aztec successors resorted to draconian human sacrifices when faced with irregular solar and lunar events. They were afraid of irregularity from the heavens.

Caste and predictability

The Hindus of India very early incorporated an elaborate caste system in their religion as a means of creating stability. Everyone would know their place and their limits and social order would be guaranteed. It is also possible that this system was designed to protect the Aryan invaders from the diseases prevalent among the native peoples of India's tropical incubator. William H. McNeill's *Plagues and Peoples* presents this fascinating hypothesis and it seems very credible. [O'Neill, *Plagues,* 92–94] The Aryans certainly did not have the disease science of today, but they tried to protect themselves by strict apartheid.

The caste system endures, despite its bankruptcy in the modern world and despite India's secular government making it illegal.

During the chaotic and confusing flight of the Hebrews from their Egyptian captivity, the Bible stories indicate that Moses was obsessed with creating order. The tribal system was set up giving the plum benefit of priestly monopoly to the Levites. To establish a sort of feudalism under the imprimaturs of God gives such a system life long beyond its utility. The ultra-Orthodox in Israel today have banned Levites (or Cohens) from marrying divorced women. Secular Israelis consider this a ridiculous archaism, as is much else connected with ultra-Orthodoxy, but no one has yet managed to unseat this powerful group.

The chaos of the collapse of Rome and barbarian invasions challenged early Christianity to reestablish order. As Rome, with its long history of law and order vanished, regional warlords were all that stood between order and anarchy. Christian thinkers came up with "the Great Chain of Being," a blueprint for feudalism that identified a hierarchy that began with God the Father and the various heavenly hosts down to kings, feudal lords, merchants, laborers, and slaves—each owing religious allegiance to the power above him.

Christian feudalism bears a striking resemblance to the Hindu caste system, with the exception of one wild card: the church hierarchy itself. Merit could (although with difficulty) propel a worthy lower caste youth (male or female) into positions of power in such institutions as convents and monasteries.

In the aftermath of the Black Death and the misguided principle of celibacy, the Catholic Church revised its message. The Old Testament command of "Be Fruitful and Multiply" was preached far and wide in the hope of bringing back a population that had been decimated. This policy is a ball and chain on Catholics to this very day, especially in the overpopulated parts of the world that do not need such a message.

Seasonal ritual

The global round of religious holidays is tied into seasons that come more or less predictably. These ties to the earth are the oldest elements of religion since the advent of agriculture, some ten thousand years ago. We depend upon the seasons, the rains, the sunshine, the right succession of temperatures, if we are to feed ourselves. In addition, the dependable cycle of seasons and religious festivals helps us to deal with the cycle of human life and our own deaths.

When the seasons are not predictable, when there is a long phase of too much winter, unseasonable rain that produces deadly rot on grain (as in the fifteenth century), or no rains for years and years (as in Mesoamerica and the American southwest), religions frantically search for a reason.

Human trust in traditional religion falters when devastating events shake people's faith in predictability. Deadly and repeated plagues or sudden or prolonged changes in climate devastate the existing power structure (both religious and civil) and new forces rush in to fill the vacuum. We can track such events in history now and should be looking at our present world, which is showing signs of similar distress.

Population explosion and implosion

The orderly continuity of human systems depends upon population stability. For most of human history, the birthrate and death rate were fairly stable. We are talking here about the thousands of years of hunting and gathering before the advent of agriculture. That mode of existence not only required socially transmitted skills, but also necessitated limiting and spacing the number of offspring when nature did not take care of the problem through infant mortality.

It is no surprise that during the difficult period of the last Ice Age, the predominant religious fixation was with fertility. The little Venus goddesses have been found in the thousands throughout the Cro-Magnon territories. These people were concerned with not only human fertility and survivability but also with the fertility of the large animals they hunted for food.

Something obviously happened to Neanderthal population numbers after thousands of years of survival. With the arrival of our ancestors, the Cro-Magnons, the Neanderthal population imploded and then vanished.

Agricultural revolution

The transformation of the human economy from hunting and gathering to agriculture resulted in a population explosion. Agriculture provided for storable foodstuffs, more calories, and stability. It also provided for the accumulation of wealth.

People could stay in one location, which made for the beginning of dense human settlements. From temporary villages, humankind graduated to permanent villages, towns, and eventually cities boasting a division of labor. Human beings no longer had to be masters of all trades, as the hunter/gatherers had been.

This transformation in human survival also transformed religion. While the Fertility Goddess was still enormously important (again, for humans and for their herds and crops), a new kind of deity appeared: the war god. When crops and herds can be stored, they are a source of wealth and a temptation to some of those hunter/gatherers who found it easier to take this wealth than to work for it. War was born.

Migratory hunter/gatherers knew fighting before agriculture evolved, but their struggles were for the protection of hunting turf, the need to drive off trespassers, not to conquer or take slaves. They had enough trouble feeding the mouths at hand.

With the advent of agriculture, trespassers were replaced by serious invaders who established a pattern that is with us in the lesser garden spots of the world today. Those still migratory peoples, herders of horses and cattle, had an advantage over the now sedentary farmers. They could arrive at harvest time and take the fruits of the farmer's labor by force. Raiding and looting was gradually replaced by conquering and staying, and religions were transformed accordingly.

Eventually, the farmers fought back. They learned to employ professional fighters to protect them against other raiders. However, the trend of history has been that the warriors prevailed. Out of this struggle came the world's aristocracies and monarchies; force shaped human civilization thereafter and down to our own time.

The Great Goddess (fertility goddesses, Venus, Isis, Virgin Mary) still had enormous following; but the revealed religions (Judaism, Christianity, Buddhism, Islam) in the forms that are *practiced* are descendants of the barbarian sky or thunderbolt war gods of antiquity. The male himself and male values are clearly enshrined in these religions, particularly in the current fundamentalist versions of all of them. They are all "muscular," and of late aggressive.

Ecology and religion

Because human beings live in and on the earth, the condition of their environment plays a large role in shaping their religions. We have already noted that the ancient Egyptians, who had a predictable annual flooding of the Nile to provide them with more than enough nourishment, had a relatively benign religion. The predictability of their lives played a role in the pyramid culture of planning for an eternity that provided the blessings of life even after death. The closest that this culture came to a war god was the desert god, a cruel deity that was constantly at war with the green world of irrigation.

For the people in the Fertile Crescent, however, life was always a struggle. They not only had unpredictable water flows from their two great rivers (Tigris and Euphrates) and much more problem with desertification, but also were an easy prey to barbarian invaders. They did not enjoy Egypt's barriers of sea and desert. They were, and still are, a superhighway across which new conquerors galloped.

The constant and vicious warfare produced a religion equally fierce. Mesopotamian gods were terrible; they were bloody and voracious, and human sacrifice played a much larger role there than in Egypt.

The Mayans and later, the Aztecs of Mexico, who certainly never heard of the gods of Mesopotamia, had an ecology similar to that of the Fertile Crescent. Drought was a genuine and cyclical threat to survival; thus what came out of the sky (rain and sun) demanded worship. Their religions were exceedingly violent, with human sacrifice playing an ever-larger role. These people also watched the skies at night for what warnings might be gleaned from the rounds of the constellations. It was not just love of knowledge that propelled Mayan astronomy; it was fear.

The ecological cycle of death and rebirth, the seeds coming up out of the earth as plants and the plants dropping seeds as they die, has its parallels in religion too. Early human farmers believed in sympathetic magic. The theory was that people could "encourage" the animals and plants by showing them what to do. A selected couple would have sex in a newly dug furrow to demonstrate fertility to their livestock or plants. May festivals in which young people danced around Maypoles were an ancient phallic worship. Young people swung on ropes and performed jumping dances to demonstrate to plants how to come up out of the ground. These things are still done in remote villages around the world.

Human sacrifice was employed—more often in desperate times than when nature was more predictable—to placate the Fertility Goddess. Such notions of sacrifice, however, permeate much later religions. One of the Greek "mystery" religions was the cult of Dionysus, the god of wine, in which sacrifice played a role. The notion of violent dismemberment and internment in the earth was acted out in imitation of the severe pruning of the dead-looking grapevines after harvest.

Of course, in the spring the dead-looking vines come back to life and bear the grape. Death and Resurrection is a central theme not just in Christianity—all religions have the notion of something of us living on after death. The scope of this belief ranges from reincarnation in Hinduism and Buddhism to Paradise in Christianity, Judaism, and Islam. Nature is the model; our religions are the reflection.

Population pressures

The introduction of new technologies such as agriculture causes human populations to explode. When there is enough food, and technologies permit us to extend our abilities (transportation, tools, irrigation, writing), our numbers increase to the point of putting too much stress on the ecology, at which point populations crash.

Population explosion is eventually followed by shortages of food, water, and such natural resources as forest, with a resultant effect on human behavior. Shortages make people desperate, and desperation breeds abrupt changes in society. The strong move in where the weak are faltering. Most of the barbarian invasions throughout history were triggered by ecological changes in the grasslands and corresponding weaknesses in population centers. The old, stable agrarian religions are often the victims of change, too, when the barbarians come in and stay.

Another ecological effect on population explosion is plague, the partner of trade and warfare. Most of the worst plagues that decimate or sometimes reduce by half civilized populations came out of the world's incubators, jungles in tropical India and southern China, and then headed west, finding dense city populations hospitable. [O'Neill: *Plagues and Peoples*]

Another incubator is Africa, which has played a role in past plagues and is now a virtual nursery for all sorts of new diseases and mutated older diseases. This incubator is now an airplane ride away from us all.

When populations are increasing and things are going well, religion plays the role of stabilizer; it gets public support to keep things as they are. However, when disaster strikes and a population plummets, people at first grow anxious and then angry at the lack of response from their gods. If the religion can quickly find a scapegoat to blame for the problem, it can survive. The famous stories of Oedipus and King David illustrate the benefits of a scapegoat. If the respective kings and their sins can be pinpointed as the cause of the plague, by the time they repent, the plague abates, and the religion is saved.

But one does not have to look back to antiquity to find scapegoats. During the thirteenth-century Black Death, Jews were the target of Christian rage in Germany, France, and Spain. Rumors were spread that Jews were poisoning the wells or were sacrificing Christian babies. The pogroms played out at last when the plague did not abate, and Jews were dying in the same numbers as Christians.

There have been times in history when the existing religion fails to save itself and is replaced. It takes a considerable cataclysm to make a religion fail, however, and our modern religions have an effective out: "God's Will." The ancients expected much more direct response from their many gods, and that excuse would not have worked.

Christianity received its first boost when the long-successful Roman civilization began to fall. Rome's collapse was ecologically driven; too many people were putting too much pressure on the agricultural land, which began to fail. As the population rapidly declined, the Roman army was obliged to draft more farmers from the land, which largely destroyed Italy's farming, and began to deplete the lands all around the Mediterranean.

Then as Rome's civilian population continued to fall, the swamps that had once been drained returned, and with them, malaria, which further reduced the population.

However, the ancient gods and goddesses continued to be supported until miseries were compounded with barbarian invasions and a series of deadly plagues. Christianity provided three things: the charity of hospitals (which Paganism did not), the promise of paradise after death, and the resignation of "God's will," a concept that sidesteps all cause and effect on the part of people.

Even the barbarians who eventually overwhelmed the Roman world were lured into Christianity because they too were up against recurrent plagues, dropping populations, and chaos. The Christian promise of life after death attracted them. They, in turn, transformed Christianity into a religion both muscular and militant, as can be seen by the time of the Crusades. It was the recently barbarian Christians who fought in those wars.

Islam was given the same boost by the ecological collapse of the late Roman world and the Persian Empire. The first Muslims were barbarian invaders, this time from the desert instead of the Central Asian grasslands. In Persia, the quick collapse of that civilization was unexpected, but the years of population explosion, armies levied to protect the Empire from the eastern barbarians, a series of deadly plagues, and the exhaustion of the peasantry who were carrying much too much burden, paved the way.

Islam replaced Persia's ancient Zoroastrianism because it demonstrated success, it preached equality (vs. the aristocracy and feudalism of Imperial Zoroastrianism), and it too could fall back on "God's Will" when there were no other answers.

Later in history, the recurrent and devastating cycles of Black Death resulted in another religious transformation: the end of the Catholic monopoly on Christianity and the birth of Protestantism and its reforms.

The Black Death had appeared first in the sixth century (more about that below) and returned to Europe with particular virulence in the 1330s. There was already an ecological issue: a failure of the heavy clay agricultural land that had been brought into grain cultivation in the tenth century with the invention of the heavy plow. By the beginning of the thirteenth century, there was a period of increased cold and rainfall and crop failures. Hunger predisposes human beings for infectious diseases. [The book to read is Robert S. Gottfried's *The Black Death*]

The expanded trade routes and the long period of the Crusades in the Middle East agricultural land set large groups of people and goods moving from Europe to China and back. Traveling with the merchant and war ships were the black rats that carried the Black Plague fleas.

This devastating plague returned again and again for the next three centuries, scarcely permitting a generation to recover from the terrible death toll before the next round came. Europe's population plummeted. This resulted in a shortage of priests, doctors, and even laborers, all of which affected social and political change in Western Europe.

The Catholic Church attempted to raise badly needed funds from a variety of dubious offers: "Indulgences" for money (buying forgiveness for sin); selling all sorts of holy relics to the gullible; and, of course, selling offices for church positions of power.

With the shortage of candidates for the priesthood, more illiterates and incompetents were recruited, a fact that was not lost on their parishes. The same problem afflicted the recruitment of nuns into convents, with a corresponding drop in the medical care these institutions offered.

The Church's monopoly was finally broken in the sixteenth century by once-priest Luther and by once-Catholic Henry VIII. The "protest" movement of Protestantism was born and almost immediately fragmented into ever more discrete sects. There was no longer just one way to be Christian, down to our own day.

Eastern Orthodox Christianity in Russia did not go through this process for a variety of historic and ecological reasons, one of them being much less population density than in Western Europe. Orthodoxy's equivalent of a protest movement was the work of one man, Czar Peter the Great, who knew he had to break the hold of the arch-conservative church if modernization were to take place. He created "New Believers" and relegated the "Old Believers" to the periphery of Russia.

The Aztecs of Mexico had a religion that had been with them for a long time: a religion with many holidays, such as the festival of the Corn Goddess, and many other violent holidays in which hundreds of human victims were sacrificed to placate the gods. The five days at the end of each year's calendar were thought to be fraught with danger, the world's very existence at stake. No one lit fires, bathed, had sex, or did anything to call attention to themselves. It was a time of total fear. [The book to read is Brian M. Fagan's *Kingdoms of Gold, Kingdoms of Jade*]

To be sure, when the Spanish arrived and the Aztec world collapsed, the Spaniards were very heavy-handed in converting the Indians. However, many of these Indians had totally lost faith in their old gods, who appeared impotent in protecting them from the horrors that Spain brought.

Furthermore, their long-held tenet that human sacrifice was obligatory to prevent the gods from destroying the world was put to the test by Spain, and the Aztec religion was proven wrong; the sun continued to rise without help from their grisly rituals. This certainly affected the conversion of Aztecs and other Mexican Indians to Catholicism.

It was not the first time that the old gods were challenged, however. Here we must look at a remarkable bit of historic detective work: a book called *Catastrophe: A Quest for the Origins of the Modern World*, by David Keys (Ballantine Books, 1999).

Keys notes that in the middle of the sixth century AD, something happened that was the natural equivalent of what scientists feared would befall the world's climate in the event of an all-out nuclear war: a "nuclear winter." Something happened that cast such a vast quantity of pulverized debris, dust, and temporarily vaporized earth into the atmosphere that the resulting barrier kept much of the sun's light and heat from the earth. Temperatures fell, the world's climate system was thrown into chaos, and famine was followed by epidemics.

Keys first tracks indications of such an event throughout the world, including ice core and tree ring evidence of the exact period in which something happened to launch this catastrophe. The event appears to have been a massive volcanic eruption in Java that actually split that island in two. The sound of this eruption carried for thousands of miles into China, where it was noted. After the explosion, there was a rain of yellow dust, a dimming of the sun for as long as a decade, and even snow in southern China in August. The Chinese, who kept good records, noted the date of the event as somewhere between November and December of 535 AD. [Keys, 150]

Plague always follows on the heels of climatic catastrophes. The climate change affects grasslands, animal populations, and human populations. Keys tracks the first arrival of the Black Death (Bubonic Plague) from Yemen to Europe, which laid the Byzantine Empire so low that the central Asian barbarians (Avars) finally were able to make the inroads that forever changed the ethnic and political geography of modern eastern Europe.

The effects of the Black Death plague of 542 on Visigothic Spain caused substantial social, economic, and political destruction. It seems to have upset the balance of power between the Visigothic ruling class and their Romano-Spanish subjects for the next century, paving the way for the Muslim invasion. The Muslims filled the vacuum and ruled Spain for the next 800 years. [Keys, 138]

The Visigoths had become impoverished by the loss of tax revenue because both taxpayers and tax collectors were killed by the plague. In addition, plague wiped out individuals of great personal, political, and military power. "In history, the creation of an abnormally large number of vacancies at the top most frequently creates a large bout of competitive—and often violent—activity to fill them."

Although Keys does not talk about this, the unexpected fall of the Persian Sassanian Empire to the invading Muslim Arabs was also a case of the shifting of the balance of power between civilized and barbarian hordes. Plague and agricultural failure devastate civilization and set it up for collapse, at which point tougher folk move in, and religions undergo change.

Japan too has a record of the change following this ecological catastrophe. The major chronicle of early Japan, the Nihon Shoki, in 536 stated: "Food is the basis of the empire. Yellow gold and ten thousand strings of cash cannot cure hunger. What avails a thousand boxes of pearls to him who is starving and cold?"

Keys notes that "...climatic catastrophe was translated into massive political and religious change through four key interrelated factors: climate, migration, disease, and religion." [Keys, 172]

Patterns of drought were followed by intense famine. Famines forced their desperately hungry victims to move around, often traveling substantial distances in search of food—and then to congregate at those few places where food or water was still available.

Just as Europe, the Middle East, and the Orient had experienced massive geopolitical change in the century following the climatic disasters of the 530s, so too did the Americas. [Keys, 183] Both in Mesoamerica and the Andes, there was a total geopolitical realignment, driven ultimately by the engine of climatic change. Keyes takes on one of history's most puzzling mysteries: the desertion of a major Mesoamerican city, Teotihuacan, centuries before even the Aztecs arrived.

An analysis of more than 150 skeletons from Teotihuacan by a forensic anthropologist shows that in the years prior to the collapse of the city-state, people began to die at an earlier age—probably because of the great drought and agricultural failure.

"Indeed the death rates for those under twenty-five virtually doubled—68.3 percent of the working-class population were dying before the age of twenty-five, compared to 38.5 percent in more normal times." [Keys, 192]

Infectious disease was always common in Teotihuacan, but when the agricultural system failed, infection increased. High death rates in the city created demand for new laborers. The countryside would have migrated to the metropolis, bringing people even less immune to city diseases. Food shortages made things worse.

Religion again failed these people. The major deities—Tlaloc, the feathered serpent Quetzalcoatl, and the Mother of Stone—were all associated with rain. When rains failed and continued to fail (maybe for several decades), there was inevitably a crisis in religious confidence.

Government was considered to be of divine origin. With failure of the gods, the leaders, too, look bad. A violent revolution broke out and the feelings of the revolutionaries were evident in the destruction of the gods' statues, as well as the very personal destruction of the elite governing class. People were murdered en masse and their bodies violated. [Keys, 193]

Andean civilization was plagued at this same time by devastating flooding (something we have been seeing in our own time). A fascinating Andean myth has come down to us from that time: God sent a terrible flood that destroyed all living things except for one man and one woman. This couple—the sole remnants of original creation—floated on the waters in a boat, and as the flood began to recede they were finally blown by the wind to a high plateau between the eastern and western sierras of the Andes. This is, of course, Lake Titicaca, the homeland of the later Inca tribe, which formed the Inca Empire in the twelfth century. [Keys, 227].

Why should we care about this catastrophe of 535? Keys has shown the ramifications of a terrible event that impacted human history for centuries. We need to be reminded that we live on a planet where such events are still possible. We could have done it to ourselves with a nuclear war. Global warming is a phenomenon that is cyclical and is apparently upon us right now. And the increase in earthquake and volcanic activity is apparent around the world. How could such events affect religious and political life? We simply need to look to the past.

Keys notes: "The 535 eruption was, as near as can be determined, one of the largest volcanic events of the past fifty thousand years. Whether looked at in terms of short- and medium-term climatic effects, caldera size (assuming proto-Krakatoa was the culprit), or ice-core evidence, the eruption was of truly mammoth proportions.

"Climatologically, the tree-ring evidence shows that it was the worst worldwide event in tree-ring record. Looking at the ice cores, we see that it may well have been the largest event to show up in both northern and southern ice caps for the past two thousand years." [Keys, 267]

Keyes looks at today's tectonic status around the world. Yellowstone and Long Valley in California are key candidates in the US. Pompeii is another. There would not be much advance notice, but the climatic effects would be enormous.

One possible consequence could be a reduction of the power of the developed world, thus opening up opportunities for the Third World.

"As the evidence in this book has demonstrated, climate has the potential to change history—not just on a short-term basis but in the long term as well. Volcanic activity is merely one of the triggers that can change climate and wield such power. Global warming (due to increased atmospheric pollution), sunspot activity, meteor or comet impacts, periodic small changes in the shape of the earth's orbit, and minor changes in the earth's axis of rotation are all capable of triggering dramatic changes in climate—and human history." [Keys, 279]

We are already seeing religious crises around the world. Population explosion followed by disease and agricultural failure is already plaguing Africa and Pakistan, as well as northern India, with predictable results.

Rising seawaters and floods from the deforested Himalayas are destroying the already marginal Bangladesh. Indonesia is next to be impacted by rising sea levels, as are all Pacific islands. Note how fanatical religion becomes the predominant issue in places facing such ecological crises.

Unlike such crises in the past, which were not understood, we human beings now do have the capacity to understand what is happening and to do something about it. We now have the scientific and rational tools to protect ourselves and to survive. But we must expect an upsurge of the irrational from human beings without these mental instruments and must be prepared to protect ourselves and our world.

It would be sheer folly to think that the Dark Ages couldn't come back.

Those who cannot remember the past are condemned to fulfill it.
—George Santayana, 1863–1952

Chapter 9.
Historic perspective

We are obviously living at the end of an era and the beginning of a new one. Historians are already noting that the Industrial Revolution that launched our era is no longer the leading edge of thought and action. We are now clearly at the beginnings of the biogenetic revolution, in which scientists use the poetic metaphor of religious terminology to say "we are reading God's blueprint for creation."

What makes times of transition so dangerous is that the various groups of the human community are not reading from the same page. There is a comparatively thin elite who think, who change, who adapt to new ideas, and who confront all human institutions that will be impacted by the new knowledge. However, this elite does not enjoy the respect of the masses of humanity, whose hearts and minds are in a completely different place.

Although democracy is not doing much better with the new ideas than the old autocracies did, the elite has been promoting democracy around the world. The masses, however, who do not understand the duties as well as the privileges of democracy, are everywhere prey to demagogues, political or religious. Today, the great challenge comes from medieval religious notions armed with modern weapons of mass destruction.

It is not difficult to sympathize with so many millions of people who would just appreciate the stability of enough food, enough order and safety, and enough predictability to lead their lives with dignity and tranquility. The world's elite have these blessings, and, to give them credit, they would like to see everyone have it.

But it is not only the downtrodden in Africa, in India, in the Middle East, and the Andes who live in chaos. The elite in the United

States and Europe have somehow failed to inspire their own ordinary citizens to trust that the new knowledge can produce something better for their lives. Until recently, Americans were accustomed to think of change as something positive—"Newer and Better"—but this vote of support can no longer be assured. Attacks on the new technologies and sciences come from both the far left and the far right.

The world is awash in cynicism, in rebellion, and in old messages of salvation—a salvation that never worked even the first time around. There is an illusion that old-time religion (including an extreme romanticization of primitivism by the left) is the answer to all problems. We don't know what consequences this will have for survival of civilization on this planet. Has this happened before?

Historic precedent

Historians are hard at work exploring what happened when organized societies were subjected to the stress of great change. If the civilization is strong enough internally, it can absorb barbarian invasions and transform the invaders into either civilized rulers or new subjects.

1200 BC crashes

About 1200 BC, a number of our most ancient civilizations were challenged and some of them fell forever. Something happened, at least across the Eurasian landmass, that affected a movement of peoples that still remains unexplored. We may be able to apply what we know about the sixth-century AD trauma (see Chapter 8) and find evidence of something similar during 1200 BC.

The Egyptians and the Sumerians, our earliest great civilizations in the Fertile Crescent, were strong enough to absorb and transform invaders for a long time.

Harrapa

A third ancient civilization, however, the Harrapan in northwest India, was totally overrun by the Aryan invaders and its demise was followed by a long dark age. The only trace of that glorious Harrapan civilization can be seen through archeology: advanced cities with water systems and sewage, with every indication of vibrant middle-class neighborhoods, high level artisan craft, and international trade. Its present-day descendant, Pakistan, is nowhere near that excellence today. What

was it like when such a civilization was brought down by the sword—
or perhaps initially by climate change?

Ancient Crete

The remarkably advanced ancient Minoan civilization in Crete was
brought down by a combination of internal revolt, external attack, and
an enormous earthquake that was followed by a seven hundred year dark
age that ended only when Greek society started to blossom.

After that first round of collapses in 1200 BC, other civilizations
underwent similar stress. China, as old and continuous as it is, had
many periods of devastating invasions, civil wars, and destruction. It
managed, however, to have numerous rebirths that restored its high
level of culture until the sixteenth century, when it went into a backward trajectory that lasted through the Communist Revolution of the
mid-twentieth century. It is now once again reasserting its genius, but
bearing the dreadful burden of centuries of neglect.

Rome

When Rome collapsed in the fourth century AD, the whole western Roman world descended into a dark barbarian age from which it
took centuries to recover. Sanitation and safe water systems that were
the hallmark of Roman civilization were the first to go, and with them
went Rome's long period of respectable public health. Papyrus from
Egypt was the next thing to vanish, and with it Rome's famed literacy.

Persia

Ancient Persia, home to three important ancient empires
(Achaemenian from the sixth century to the fourth century BC, Parthian
from the third century BC to the third century AD, and Sasanian from
the third century to the seventh century AD), underwent numerous
invasions and collapses, each followed by recovery and renaissance,
much like China. The culture was so strong and civilized that it could
withstand most—but not all—disasters.

Alexander the Great was the first disaster for Persia. Most of us
trained in Western scholarship have a soft spot for Alexander, the
Macedonian barbarian who was educated by Aristotle and who conquered an enormous empire before his death at 33. His legend—that
of being the Philosopher King—gives him much more credit than he
deserves. His army's rapine and destruction of Persian Zoroastrian texts,

priests, and temples as he cut a swath through Persia devastated Persia's religious culture for centuries to come, although their political culture recovered. [The book to read is Mary Boyce, "A History of Zoroastrianism," *Handbuch der Orientalistik*, Vol. 1, Leiden/Koln, E. J. Brill, 1975]

In the seventh century AD, as described in Chapter 8, another wave of barbarians transformed the face of civilizations. The new sect of Islam swept out of Arabia and both took down and then absorbed the civilization of the Persians and much of Byzantium, creating a brief dark age that was soon followed by a golden age that swept the world from Spain to the gates of China.

The Arab Muslim assault on Persia had mixed consequences, however. The imperial, technological, and intellectual/artistic culture of Persia was absorbed by the Arabs and within short order, it became the basis for Islam's Golden Age when the Caliphate moved to Baghdad. The ancient religious culture of Persia did not fare as well. Islam proved to be the fatal blow to a religion that had illuminated three successive Persian empires and its people for more than 1000 years. [Farhat-Holzman, *Strange Birds from Zoroaster's Nest.*]

The most devastating barbarian invasion of Persia, the Mongol assault of the thirteenth century, reduced the population by half and destroyed so much of the civilized infrastructure of the country that Persia never quite recovered. It has remained depressed and pessimistic since that time, and a fanatical Turkic barbarian takeover (the Safavids) two centuries later brought with it the Shi'a sect of Islam, which thrives on resentment and pessimism.

It is apparent that cataclysms, whether man-made or geological/biological can bring civilized cultures to their knees and can have transforming effects on religion.

Civilizations and dark ages

Am I being judgmental in calling barbarian periods "dark ages?" Perhaps so. Defenders of the barbarians note their vigorous manliness and rough egalitarianism and compare this with the decadence of civilizations. They have a point. But perhaps the rapidity with which conquering barbarians take to civilization's decadences says something about civilization's appeal.

There are standards that almost all great civilizations considered important to their success—and when they violated their own standards, they invited disaster. The standards include urban cleanliness and order, safe water and concern for sewage disposal, the well-being of the food growers and a large surplus of food to nourish cities, the well-being of craftsmen and support for a healthy and wide-ranging trade system, and the perception by the public that their government was competent, benevolent, and could protect them.

Civilizations at their best uphold these standards. However, over time, defense issues (or that old nemesis, graft) overwhelm the civilian institutions and the system becomes thin and vulnerable. The cost of defense increases to such an extent that the peasants are exhausted and the artisans and traders taxed to penury.

Barbarians from Asia

Barbarians regarded civilizations as rich pickings, and after repeated challenges to the muscle of a civilization to defend itself, the barbarians prevailed. How the new political and cultural order emerged depended on the underlying strength or weakness of the conquered civilization.

For example, when the barbarians conquered the late Roman Empire in Italy, the society was already in steep decline. The population had begun to crash, literacy was in decline, and even order and cleanliness were on the run.

The barbarian invasions, from Italy through France and Spain, resulted in a loss of civilized values. Christian recruitment benefited from the despair of people who saw their bright societies going dark, but also suffered from the barbarian savagery that infused it, particularly in Spain. A real dark age settled on the former Roman Empire and did not brighten until contact with the Muslims in the invasion of Spain (711 AD) and later during the First Crusade (1098 AD).

Arabs

The Arabs, who began as barbarian invaders, took large territories of the Byzantine Greco-Roman world beginning about 611 AD and the Sassanian Persian Empire in 651, both of which had been high civilizations, but were exhausted from warfare against each other, and against the central Asian barbarians.

With the defense burden lifted, these two bright cultures gave the eager Arabs something that they had not had before—sophisticated empire (and a life of the mind from the Persians). The Arab barbarians gave their conquered territories a unifying and (for that time) liberal and relatively tolerant religion. The dark age was short, and the subsequent Muslim Golden Age (about 800 AD) dazzling.

Mongols

Even those most deadly barbarians, the Mongols of Genghis Khan, who actually debated whether their duty was to destroy cities, those sinkholes of iniquity, relented. They destroyed plenty of cities, but then were themselves seduced by the charms of civilization. Cleanliness, beautiful women, great art, and the luxuries of international trade finally brought them into the mainstream of society.

In Persia, after destroying nearly half of the country, they revived Persian culture and actually restored Persian national identity for the first time since the Muslim invasion. The Mongols became Muslim in Iran and Buddhist in China; cohesive empire was more important to them than religion.

Spanish conquistadors

The last barbarian invasion we will explore here is the Spanish conquest of the Aztecs and Incas of the New World. It may seem irregular to count the Christian Spaniards, with their guns and steel, as barbarians, yet they certainly meet the standard definition given by the Prophet Zoroaster, some 1200 years BC: people who do not plant, do not craft, but think they have the right to take the fruits of others' labor. Zoroaster considered the barbarians of his time as masters of the great lie. The Spaniards qualified.

They descended on two civilizations of considerable quality: clean, orderly, productive of both food and trade goods. The Spaniards did what the Muslim invaders did: they replaced the top level of governance with themselves, and, at least at first, left all other strata in place. Then they tried to replace the indigenous religions with Christianity with mixed success.

What truly devastated both conquered peoples was the combination of Old World plagues, to which the natives had no immunity, enslavement in mining, and ruthless looting and confiscatory taxing of the great wealth these civilizations had accumulated. The Spanish took much, gave little, and after a brief period of conspicuous consumption, even Spain became a backwater.

Aztec Mexico and Incan Peru, Bolivia, and Ecuador, sank into the misery from which it has been difficult to recover. Nor did their new religion make things better. Catholicism was firmly entrenched with the ruling oligarchy, and its function was to keep the populace docile.

Progress or reaction

We in the West are inclined to view history and time as more or less linear. Progress is an entrenched concept for us, in contrast to that of much of the traditional world, which sees cycles instead. Hinduism and Buddhism conceive of endless rounds of life, death, and rebirth— much as can be seen from the cycles of vegetative and animal life around us. Progress had not been a consideration until contact with the West.

The fifteenth-century discovery of the hitherto unknown Western Hemisphere, the seventeenth-century religious revolutions, the eighteenth-century industrial revolution and enormous social and political changes, and the nineteenth- and twentieth-century growth of secular governance and explosions in scientific knowledge, have made it seem to us that we were continually moving toward new ways of organizing human life.

It is very difficult for those of us who believe in progress to imagine going backwards, yet it can and has happened many times before in human history. I read with a shiver of recognition Jared Diamond's *Guns, Germs, and Steel* [Diamond] in which he tracked the fortunes of the Polynesians who set out from Asia with the same artifacts: pigs, the yam, agricultural and fishing tools, and other things needed for agricultural life. Some of these voyagers found themselves on islands not amenable to agriculture, and before long they lost the arts and reverted to hunting and gathering. One indeed can go backwards.

What must it be like for the people living in a crashing civilization who still remember the good times?

Spain

Spain, during its Muslim Golden Age, was a thriving society with effective agriculture, strong international trade, skilled craftsmen, and vibrant scientific and cultural establishments. Islam in those days was a catalyst for religious toleration of Christians and Jews, a patron for the scientific and cultural elites, and an aid to international trade. People living under that governance (800–1200 AD) probably could not imagine the Spain of 1600, in which the Christians regained control and drove out or forcibly converted the Muslims and Jews. Christians managed—in one century of dreadful governance—to empty the cornucopia that Spain had once been.

Spain's agriculture was devastated and was replaced by sheep herding, which is always a bad economic sign. The Spanish crafts of metallurgy, leather, textiles, and even book production left with the Muslims. The intellectual excellence of Spain was nipped in the bud by the expulsion of both Jews and Muslims and the suffocating grip of Spain's restored "muscular Christianity." There is nothing like an Inquisition to halt all thought or drive it into exile. (The book to read is Americo Castro's *The Spaniards*.)

The Muslims were not without blame for Spain's catastrophe, either. Between 1200 and 1492 AD, Muslims fought among themselves, found their world trade networks cut off during the Mongol siege of Asia, and were also victims of the Black Death that devastated Europe. One more wave of Muslims assaulted Spain from North Africa, this time bringing not enlightenment, but fanaticism.

This second Moorish wave was ignorant, vicious, and had a variety of Islam not unlike that of the recent Taliban in Afghanistan. They shut down intellectual activity and attributed the plagues and other catastrophes to God's wrath, which could only be remedied by strict adherence to their notion of Islam.

These actions set the stage for the return of the Spanish Christians, who picked up where the second Moorish invasion left off. Religious conformity was the state's most pressing issue, and Christians relentlessly pursued it, to Spain's long-lasting damage.

Sub-Saharan Africa

What is it like in today's sub-Saharan Africa, now freed from the oppressive colonial rule of the European powers? What must it be like for a Nigerian educated at Oxford or Cambridge to watch his recently minted country come apart from incompetent home rule? What has become of the road system, the water system, the educational system, the public health agencies, and the civil service that the colonialists had established (and that the Nigerians certainly liked)? This same dire scenario is unfolding elsewhere in formerly colonial Africa.

Rational governance is being replaced by an explosion of religious fundamentalism. Nigeria is quickly heading for religious wars between the northern Islamists and the burgeoning Christian south. [See *Newsweek*, 4/16/01 and *CSM*, 1/4/01] One can find the same myopic literalism in both camps.

There are Christian groups that organize around faith healing and charismatic hysteria—strong elements among pre-Christian tribal religions. Others look to all biblical references of witchcraft and the supernatural—again, tribal religious obsessions. Yet others look to Christianity to provide the wealth and success so evident in the Christian West.

The Islamists are fixated on the sexual promiscuity that characterizes modernizing African life. At the same time, they look to what they consider Islam's support of polygamy and the cloistering of women. Vigilante Muslim groups are tearing around the countryside shutting down places of entertainment such as cinemas, restaurants, and nightclubs where both men and women meet, and they are also insisting upon sexually segregated workplaces.

Neither group of religious enthusiasts is the least sympathetic to democracy. Muslim groups are already going after each other—and it will not be long before Christian groups do the same. This does not bode well for rational governance and a prospering secular society.

Indonesia traveled in a fifty-year period from repressive Dutch rule to independent nationhood that attempted to create a modern state where there had been no sense of national identity before. As long as the country continued to educate its children in a common language, develop its natural resources, and develop Indonesia's first genuine middle-class, it seemed to flourish. This was all achieved under a repressive but effective dictatorship—until financial corruption caught up with it.

With the economic crash of the over-extended stock and bond markets in Asia (a crisis of banking and political cronyism, really), the dictatorship started to come apart. Irate middle class citizens began to agitate for participation in their own governance, hopefully in a democratic fashion.

This confluence of disasters was almost too much for the fragile new state. Island regions that provided much of the natural wealth had been despoiled and the needs of the residents neglected. The military dictatorship that had held all this together foundered, and until recently it looked as if the country would break apart.

Indonesia came close to having a dark age descend upon it. Not only was the infrastructure crumbling, but worse yet, ethnic antipathies that had been suppressed by the nationalist government rose to the surface, largely clothed in religious fanaticism. Islam, which previously had a relatively mild face in Indonesia, has suffered an infusion of Saudi money and new and fanatical Islamism. Christians in more remote islands have been under siege. But Christian converts can also be ugly. The Dyak tribesmen of Borneo revived their ancient custom of headhunting—they decapitated 500 Muslim neighbors, not necessarily because they were Muslim, perhaps, but because they were unwanted immigrants.

To everyone's surprise, the middle class has rallied and two decent democratic elections have taken place. They appear to be in recovery. Today's government is gingerly taking on Muslim terrorists in court, spurred by several very nasty terrorist attacks aimed at tourists, and at foreigners living in Indonesia.

Our own fate

What are the dangers for those of us in the developed societies of the world? Have we developed so solidly that we cannot fall back to a darker age? What stresses on our civilization have occurred before with disastrous consequences?

Ecological

The connections between human actions and the natural world have been forcefully brought to our awareness, beginning with Rachel Carson's landmark work, *Silent Spring*. Human-caused ecological problems are often the result of good intentions but unforeseen consequences. The use of the insecticide DDT was such a case, and, in its effectiveness against fleas and mosquitoes, we overlooked its effect on birds and other insectivores. We now know better.

Our decent concern for human life has raised the longevity of most of us through improved sanitation and effective medicines, and has lowered infant mortality. Laudable as this seems, it has contributed to a global population explosion with dire results. There are more people struggling for life on this planet than ever before in human history, and the majority are living in increasing misery. To compound the problem, rational considerations are sacrificed to conservative religious notions posing as "the sanctity of life" but which are in reality the religious control of sexuality. The United States, a developed country that should know better, shows official hostility to population control.

What are the ramifications of this population explosion?

Social

- Poverty and violence in the Middle East have spawned Muslim terrorism.
- There has been an increase in the number of abandoned and enslaved children in Brazil, the Indian subcontinent, and Africa.
- The number of conflicts in the world has increased, particularly in Africa, with horrifying savagery, as well as in Indonesia and the Indian subcontinent.
- There has been an increase in religious hysteria and intolerance in the Middle East, Indonesia, and Africa.
- Violence against women is on the rise globally, including an upsurge of international trafficking of women for sex and slave labor.

Medical

- As in other times of population explosion and wide travel, lethal diseases are readily spread around the globe.
- Despite enormous Western medical advances, many undertreated diseases are developing resistance to all known drugs. Tuberculosis, the disease of overcrowded cities in the nineteenth century, has returned and is now once again lethal. There are international attempts at meeting this problem but they are hampered by inadequate funding.
- With increasing warfare, there is the spectre of biological warfare—a weapon used against food supply or human targets. This weapon was formerly the monopoly of developed states (western European nations, the US,

and the USSR) but is now being considered by Third World states, either dictatorial (Iraq, prior to the US invasion) or religious-fascist (Iran, Pakistan).

Ecological
- Population pressure on forests for lumber and, in poorer places, for firewood is affecting global climate.
- Flooding, a consequence of mountain deforestation, is threatening to eventually inundate Bangladesh, with a population of 141 million that has no place to flee.
- The Green Revolution that fed India for some time is showing stress. The watershed is being poisoned by the chemicals that produced the bumper crops of grain.
- Global warming may be partly a natural phenomenon, but it is being hastened by increased carbon dioxide production from human technology. This warming is changing global weather patterns and threatening crops.
- Increasing famine is weakening populations exposed to diseases. The HIV/AIDS plague in Africa is a devastating example of this.

Geological changes
- There has been a dramatic increase in volcanic and seismic activity around the world. Such activity, if severe enough, can affect climate and crop yields for a prolonged period. This has occurred on our planet before, with dire consequences of famine, disease, and political chaos.
- Comet impact is a new study that is now being spearheaded by a leading geologist/astronomer, Robert Schumaker, who discovered the comet string that impacted Jupiter in 1995. Schumaker's lifework has been devoted to exploring what were once thought to be volcanic craters, but which are now known to be the result of comet impact. One such impact was fairly recent, early in the twentieth century in Siberia. The impact set enormous forest fires, but its consequences were relatively limited.

Another comet impact recently discovered was a pre-historic collision at the tip of Yucatan Peninsula. The impact was so huge that it is thought to have wiped out the globe's dinosaurs, not slowly but within just a few years.

The likelihood of a major hit is nothing to keep us up at night, however. We are bombarded daily to little ill effect. If a big one comes, there is not much we can do about it. We will be gone. But if a medium comet hits us, the effect will be like that of a large volcanic eruption: interruption of sunlight to the earth, which can have a serious effect on agriculture, food supply, disease, and political stability.

What should concern us at this moment in human history, comets aside, is the great danger that accompanies periods of change. We are on the verge of a global culture that includes such things as our banking system, universal political participation in governance, human rights that include identification of females as human, and a modern global food and health system. If permitted to unfold, the new global culture could provide human beings with better, more just, and healthier lives than mass society has ever enjoyed before.

The obstacles to these changes come from vested interests in the older dispensations: feudal landowners; resurgent religions that feel that changes, particularly democratic and human rights changes, are by their nature evil; and by political demagogues, in both developed and Third World countries, who appeal to twisted thinking.

Countries in the lesser-developed world will fail to thrive until the population explosion plays out its dreadful scenarios (disease, ecological failure, and political anarchy), which may take at least two more decades.

The developed world faces other dangers. There is a thin elite of advanced thinkers who continue to propel us onto the next steps of cultural evolution:

- Exploration of space;
- A fuller knowledge of how the earth works (ecology);
- Genetic sciences in foods and medicines;
- Human rights that include females, homosexuals, and the physically and mentally impaired;
- A new sense of micro-community;

- A new concept of justice that includes early intervention and prevention.

Opposition to these cultural advances will not come from the large and essentially supportive middle class, but will come from the twisted thinkers, current varieties of religious literalists from all camps and the political demagogues who share their values. Fear is always a danger to clear thought.

Democracies run the risk of pandering to the lowest common denominator, for whom thinking is not a priority. Our best hope lies in reasoned thinking, humane values, and seeing to the economic health of our system, out of which comes the luxury of a great society. This is created by an elite, which unfortunately cannot outvote the ignorant.

There should be little difficulty in choosing between the fruits of our era and the fruits of the past. In our era we have astronomers leading the exploration of the universe, oceanographers discovering whole new species in the ocean depths, biogeneticists who have mapped the entire human genome system that will transform human survival, and historians who seek to understand where we have been so that we can know where we go. On the other hand, the fruits from the past offer us radical and violent Islamism, tribalism and ethnic strife, and old-fashioned savagery. With them come the three riders of the Apocalypse.

Is there a choice?

"It was the best of times—it was the worst of times..."
—Charles Dickens, *A Tale of Two Cities*

Epilogue

The words quoted above are from that favorite novel of ninth grade teachers, Charles Dickens' *A Tale of Two Cities*. I was moved by the love story at age fourteen, but did not understand Dickens' keen-eyed analysis of a revolution gone amok until adulthood and firsthand experience with another revolution (the Iranian) that indeed ran amok.

Static times do not spawn revolution; revolutions are formed much like tornadoes: from the collision of hot and cold air.

Our own revolutionary time is just the latest consequence of the four revolutions that followed the discovery of the New World: the printing press, the Industrial Revolution, the political revolutions of France and America, and the energy revolution that finally replaced the horse as our main source of energy.

In the twentieth century, several more science and technology revolutions and one social revolution have changed life on this planet forever. The scientific revolutions include man's release from earth's gravity (air and space travel), the birth-control pill, the mapping of the human genome, and the enormous promise of stem cell research.

Equally important is the social revolution that has emancipated women from 10,000 years as male property. Although space exploration and female emancipation are as yet in their infancy, earth as a great prison for so many will never be the same, despite noisy rear-guard action. The gates are ajar.

All of these changes have left many people around the world unmoored and unhinged. The Muslim suicide bombers used hijacked civilian airliners to declare war on the social aspects of modern life by murdering more than 3,000 people in the New York World Trade Center and the Pentagon in Washington. But even these religious fascists, could they prevail, would use modern weapons and technology to keep the rest of us under their control.

Living in the midst of such times puts us in the position of Dante's hero, who found himself lost in the middle of his life in the middle of a dark forest. It is difficult to know where we are. When we are inundated with world and local news that brings us civil war, ethnic strife, state torture, domestic battery and murder, and death squads eliminating homeless children as if they were vermin, it is difficult to see that we are moving into another, and possibly better, era. Yet I believe we are. The horrors listed above are old horrors, but they are now seen as unacceptable for the first time ever by a growing number of educated people around the world.

Human beings do not change age-old patterns of behavior without a fight. Real change cannot be imposed on the Third World or on our own less enlightened citizens by the developed world's elite. Nevertheless, we are slowly beginning to assume the configurations of a global society with global values. Our bad habits (tobacco and sugary soft drinks) went global in the blink of an eye. Good habits take longer to spread. Radio and television are available everywhere—as is cinema and, increasingly, the Internet. These media can be used for good purposes, entertainment, or evil.

Since the momentous venture of Columbus, which for better or worse gave us a complete picture of our blue sphere, the information revolution burst on the scene. Columbus' adventure was partnered by the invention of the printing press, which broke forever the monopoly of knowledge in the hands of the power structure. Knowledge is power.

Secrecy and conspiracies of silence are gone forever. In Europe, information was once the property of the Catholic Church. When that monopoly was lost, so was the Church's unity. Rivals sprang up, and religion is still fragmenting day by day.

In our own century, dictatorships recognized the power of information and they not only monopolized it, but also twisted such information to their own agendas—a system known as propaganda. Even commonplace information was considered dangerous. It was not long ago that the Soviet Union prohibited city maps and phone directories in

Moscow. The public was not allowed to mix and meet without Big Daddy watching.

The Chinese, too, were able to put down revolts with brutal efficiency—invisible to the rest of the world until a demonstration in Tiananmen Square was broadcast to the world via satellite, phone, and fax communications. The Chinese government no longer can take cover under a monopoly of information.

Now, in the twenty-first century, militant Islamists are using media and modern communications to propagandize their cause, while attempting to censor any ideas that they do not like. In Iran, for example, the state is in a constant battle against the press, shutting down newspapers and magazines that "insult Islam." They are also waging—but losing—a battle against satellite dishes.

There is no doubt that open information is the enemy of tyranny and oppression. But there is no guarantee that the Information Revolution is falling, like apple seeds, on prepared earth. Bill Gates, one of our century's most creative computer entrepreneurs, presents a dazzling vision of the future—a global intelligence breakthrough. He tells us what *could* happen, but is that what *will* happen?

I think a case could be made that if the ground is not prepared for those seeds, nothing may come up but trouble. An information revolution floating on high with instant communication of experts, leaving on the ground the masses of this world who have virtually no general educational and reasoning capability, may be a blueprint for disaster.

We have done better in the past. Can we imagine ourselves in the shoes of our nineteenth-century American ancestors, standing in the cold for hours, listening to the Lincoln-Douglas debates? Those ancestors were not even college educated, for the most part, but they certainly knew how to read and write and think! They understood Western history, knew the same mythology, and had a good grasp of the two most eloquent works in English: the King James translation of the Bible and the writings of William Shakespeare. They also had the patience to wade through the complexities.

Where is such an audience today? The few thoughtful people rounded up as a panel by PBS to postmortem a presidential speech or debate are a minority indeed. The vast majority of people do not or cannot read, do not have much of an attention span, and have no basis in their educations to evaluate anything beyond their narrow concerns.

Our shared common culture in this country is unraveling daily in the hands of two kinds of protesters, from the left and from the right. The protesters from the political left detest any sort of authority, and they want to punish government and flout middle-class values. The Earth Liberation Front, which sees fit to torch homes, resorts, and university science departments, is a representative of this New-Age quasi-religious fanaticism. [*SCS*, 12/07/04.]

From the right come protesters against any sort of joint global efforts, and also against female and racial equality. Under the guise of their select religious fundamentalisms, these groups make murderous raids against government facilities, officials, and abortion clinics.

How can we have a "global society" with a revival of "America Firsters" on the one side and anti-science, anti-intellectual fanatics on the other side? And, further afield than our own back yard, what happens to international communication when there are fights over whether English or French, the languages of recent colonizers, should be replaced by Swahili, the language of an older colonizer, in Africa? Does anyone suggest learning more than one language? Computer programs are available to enable almost any child to learn multiple languages, but if the society fights this, we descend into language wars.

How can we have an information revolution when human knowledge is leaping forward on every front, but is under siege by the literalists on school boards who insist on placing Biblical Creationism side by side with evolution as "alternative theories" with comparative merit? What kind of science is this?

In Africa, a Western-trained psychiatrist is compelled to share his diagnoses with "alternative" believers in sorcery, placing science in the same pickle it is in between the Creationists and Evolutionists. Where does the Information Revolution stand here?

The UN tried sending computers and software to the most remote African villages to begin the process of educating children, a process that African governments did not consider a priority. Even if electricity were widely available, which it was not, what happens when the computer learning is utterly at odds with village superstition and traditional "values?"

How does a computer program deal with female genital mutilation? Does it pass it off as an "alternative value system?"

It may be instructive to see what history tells us about previous information revolutions, and yes, there have been such. The invention of writing systems 5,000 years ago launched the first. The Phoenician alphabet launched the second. Chinese paper manufacture and Islamic literacy launched the third. The printing press launched the fourth. How did those revolutions affect mankind's potential for civilized and intellectual growth?

Three great civilizations were kept alive for a very long time thanks to their writing and communications systems. China, as old and unwieldy as it is, had been kept together by its Confucian system of learning and order, a system for command and control through writing, and an agreement on these values through all strata of society.

The Greco-Roman world remained coherent and seemingly rational for so long because there was a shared value system of custom, reason, and written law.

The Muslim Golden Age (700–1200 AD) maintained a coherent, shining civilization that cut across ethnic and national boundaries from Spain to Central Asia because that culture shared a common, comprehensible religion that valued urbanized behavior. They also shared, during those five centuries, the inherited culture of reason and law that had formerly belonged to the Greco-Roman world and the intellectual and cultural treasures of the Persian empires.

What brought all of these great civilizations to a screeching halt? Invasions of superstition and the thundering hoof beats of barbarian hordes broke the links of shared culture that had made them strong. Each suffered darkness and ignorance after their golden eras.

The Industrial Revolution and the political and literacy revolutions that accompanied it provided what has become in our own time a global civilization. This civilization, like all preceding civilizations, depends upon our being able to talk to each other in common terms. We must share values, some language of commerce, and modes of reasoning and governance. For a brief moment, it looked as if we could do this—but I am hearing the roar of superstition and thundering hoofs once more— noise from the wings that may soon gallop to center stage.

We are on the threshold of an astonishing breakthrough of human understanding. Children with a modicum of computer skill can teach themselves anything that their curiosity finds for them. A good computer and a willing child approach the old goal of Greek learning: one on one, tutor and pupil. And what a tutor! It potentially contains and can transmit all human knowledge. In addition, in the developed civilizations of today, girl children are no longer forbidden learning. This doubles the pool of intellectual talent.

But how do we deal with all the people who do not have this access and never developed intellectual curiosity? How can we deal with them if they are also vocal, rigid, and obstructive? How do we deal with democratic governance that increasingly confronts complicated issues that voters, not to mention legislators, do not understand? How will we bridge that period in our own country when the largest part of the population is computer ignorant and knowledge deficient? Of course the day will come when every child will have access to this new knowledge, but we are far from that now and without public will it will not be addressed soon.

New knowledge without some new, shared system of values has great potential for danger as well as good. How do we deal with scientific and cultural ignorance in our own very lucky country, considering what this is already costing us in intelligent governance? Where has the Space Program gone? What will we do when the next global plague hits? Why is there so little money in the science budget?

Can democracy, which we value so much, cope with emergency decision making? Some of the major problems facing our world are not being faced by the hordes of the ignorant, whose votes can be bought by demagogues with agendas. Democracy for the ignorant may be a very large mistake.

Are we on the eve of decades of chaos, warfare, barbarian raids, ecological crises, and general Tower of Babel miscommunication, as a number of pessimistic futurists predict?

How long will it take before we have a genuine world culture that is accepted as the underpinning of global values? We will need to use this Information Revolution to bring about this cultural good. It cannot be neutral. And yet I can hear the screaming protests from all the world's well-meaning but intellectually medieval reactionaries. They say: "If we go back to the good old days, if we go back to our old-time religion, everybody will know their place and be content once more." Ah, were it but that simple.

My hunch is that some major global disasters will provide the impetus for some sort of global governance, and it will not be the democracy that we have today. The barbarians (Osama bin Laden and his ilk in the world's lesser garden spots) can only destroy; they will not be the global leaders. If we are lucky, this leadership will come from the elite who know how to do things, from the worlds of business, science, and technology. Conditions will be so dire that they will not have to convince the poor and ignorant to accept their governance; it will be obvious.

To make such governance civilized and humane, however, it will take another elite that is emerging today in, of all things, public media. *Newsweek* magazine (5/21/01, 30–37) recently ran a thoughtful feature, stimulated by the execution of mass-murderer/bomber Timothy McVeigh, on "The Roots of Evil." This article explored the recent history of evil—zealots, monsters, and tyrants—and then searched out religious and secular concepts of sin and evil. I am happy to see this sort of issue explored in the popular press with such intelligence.

Of course since the September 11th attack by Osama bin Laden's cult, the media have been galvanized in an attempt to understand the psychological forces that produced this horror. Evil is certainly a major force here.

My local newspaper ran a remarkable long article from the Associated Press on "Exploring the Origins of War." The article looked to human remains of 14,000 years ago, asking whether war is genetically programmed into the human psyche. [*SCS*, 5/20/01] It is not. But the factors that generate war are now known—and religion must take a large hit. It provides the cement for a group to think its cause is divinely ordained. However, under all such rationalizations and justifications, lies the real reason for war: *too many people after too little food.*

Another surprisingly popular piece was presented by the Arts & Entertainment TV network — a two-hour program based on Karen Armstrong's *A History of God.* The participants, including Armstrong herself, were historians and theologians of great ability, and what emerged was a picture of religious evolution and almost ecumenical agreement. Fundamentalists did not attend. This represented the best and brightest of minds engaged in theology and history. From them may come the ethics and values needed by the world of the near future.

I believe that the world that we are entering will eventually wind up rational and civilized. Getting there will take us all through the valley of the shadow of death, but perhaps every revolution does that. This one will be no different.

Bibliography

Alireza, Marianne, *At the Drop of a Veil*, Blind Owl Press, 2002.

Andregg, Michael, *On the Causes of War*, Ground Zero Minnesota, 1999.

Armstrong, Karen, *Muhammad, a Biography of the Prophet*, Harper San Francisco, 1992.
——*The Battle For God*, Alfred A. Knopf, 2000.
—— *A History of God*, Ballantine Books (reprint edition), 1994.

Barzun, Jacques, *From Dawn to Decadence: 1500 to the Present, 500 Years of Western Cultural Life*, HarperCollins, 2000.

Boyce, Mary, "A History of Zoroastrianism," *Handbuch der Orientalistik*, Vol. 1 (Leiden/Koln, E. J. Brill, 1975).

Brinton, Crane, *The Anatomy of a Revolution*, Prentice-Hall, NY, 1958 (revised edition).

Brooks, Geraldine, *Nine Parts of Desire: The Hidden World of Islamic Women*, Anchor Books (Random House), 1995.

Castro, Americo, *The Spaniards, an Introduction to Their History*, University of California Press, 1971.

Clarkson, Frederick, *Eternal Hostility: The Struggle Between Theocracy and Democracy*, Common Courage Press, Monroe, Maine, 1997.

Diamond, Jared: *Guns, Germs, and Steel: The Fates of Human Societies*, W. W. Norton & Co., 1998.

Fagan, Brian M., *Kingdoms of Gold, Kingdoms of Jade: The Americas Before Columbus*, Thames & Hudson, 1991.

Farhat-Holzman, Laina, *Strange Birds From Zoroaster's Nest: An Overview of Revealed Religions*, Rev. 2nd ed., Nonetheless Press, 2003.

Goldberg, Jeffrey, "Inside Jihad U," *The New York Times Magazine*, June 25, 2000.

Gottfried, Robert S., *The Black Death: Natural and Human Disaster in Medieval Europe*, Free Press (Division of Macmillan), 1983.

Huntington, Samuel P., *Political Order in Changing Societies*, Yale University Press, 1968.

Kaplan, Robert D., "The Lawless Frontier," *The Atlantic Monthly*, September, 2000.

Keys, David, *Catastrophe: A quest for the origins of the Modern World*, Ballantine Books, 1999.

McNeill, William H., *Plagues and Peoples,* Monticello Editions, Quality Paperback Book Club, 1976.

Lewis, Bernard, Ed., *The World of Islam: Faith, People, Culture,* Thames & Hudson, 1992.
———*The Assassins: A Radical Sect in Islam*, Oxford University Press, 1967.

Lifton, Robert J., *Destroying the World to Save It: Aum Shinrikyo, Apocalyptic Violence, and the New Global Terrorism,* Metropolitan Books (Henry Holt & Co.), 1999.

McGirk, Tim, "The World of Islam," *Time Magazine*, September 28, 1998.

Nafisi, Rasool: "Opening of the Door of Ijtihad," Conference of Ancient
    and Medieval Philosophy, SUNY Binghamton, October 26, 2000.

Naipaul, V.S., *Beyond Belief: Islamic Excursions Among the Converted
    Peoples*, Random House, 1998.
——— *Among the Believers: an Islamic Journey*, Alfred A. Knopf, 1981.

Index